Physician Entrepreneurs Who Live Life And Practice Medicine On Their Own Terms

Compiled by Nneka Unachukwu

BOOKS BY NNEKA UNACHUKWU, M.D
The EntreMD Method
Made for More
The Visibility Formula
The Profitable Private Practice Playbook

Made For More 2
Physician Entrepreneurs Who Live Life and Practice Medicine on Their Own Terms

ISBN
Paperback 978-1-963503-08-1
Ebook 978-1-963503-09-8

To the students and alumni of the EntreMD Business School.

Your courage to defy the odds and build your dream businesses and dream lives makes you shining examples of what is possible.

You are the vision boards so desperately needed.

You are the cavalry the physician community has been waiting for.

CONTENTS

INTRODUCTION

You're not going to waste your valuable time on something you don't believe is possible. But, until you give it a try, how do you know if your big dream is one you can actually pull off?

You see someone else doing it.

When you chose a career in medicine, you knew it wouldn't be an easy path to get to medical school, then get *through* medical school to become a physician. But you knew it was *possible*, because you'd seen people do it.

Thousands and thousands of doctors have made it through the rigors of medical school in order to practice medicine. They're seeing patients, performing surgeries, providing healing care, and earning a good living doing it. They're proof that becoming a physician is an achievable goal.

But what if you're a physician who has even *bigger* dreams for your life and career—dreams *beyond* practicing medicine in a clinic or hospital? What if you want to start your own business and become a physician entrepreneur? What if you want the freedom to live your dream life and practice medicine on your own terms?

Is that kind of dream possible? And how can you know for sure?

You see someone else doing it.

I first dreamed of becoming a physician entrepreneur over a decade ago. But I didn't know if it was possible because I didn't see anyone else doing it. So I paved my own way. And now I've become a walking vision board for the physician community. I show them that it's possible. And I show them how to do what I've done.

This book is filled with some powerful stories from some amazing physician entrepreneurs who have worked with me, but first let me start with my own story.

My Physician Entrepreneur Origin Story

The year was 2010, and I had just started my own private practice, 15 months after residency. I also had two children under the age of two. I was nothing if not ambitious. I had big dreams, big goals, and even though I was very afraid, I was willing to go after them.

Of course, once I started my practice, I realized something: I was a physician, not an entrepreneur. I knew how to take care of my patients; I did not know how to run a business. I did not know how to get people to come through my doors. Nothing in my medical training had prepared me to run a practice that would serve well and earn well.

I was going to have to figure this out on my own. So I did.

At the time, I didn't know how to speak, how to network, or how to market myself and my business. (And did I mention those two babies?) Not only did I not have the know-how, I was a super shy, socially awkward introvert.

So I took a deep breath, dared my fears, and taught myself everything I needed to know. And, through this intense time of learning, I found my calling. I would use my experience and expertise to help other physicians become entrepreneurs, to build their dream lives and practice medicine on their terms, just like I was doing.

A few years later, EntreMD was born. I started this company in an effort to help 100,000 physicians do what I had done: build a profitable business that gave me time, freedom, fulfillment, and a lasting legacy. As the CEO of EntreMD, I lead the EntreMD Business School (EBS), host a successful podcast, write bestselling books, and speak confidently on stages around the country. We just had a multi-million dollar year, and we serve hundreds of physicians at the highest level. And EntreMD is just one of five successful companies I own.

I took my private practice to seven figures as a pediatrician—and as a mom of four children. To do what I did, while raising and homeschooling my kids, is a powerful example to the physician community. I'm living proof that they can also do big things no one thinks can be done. And I didn't just grow my private practice to seven figures. I built the systems and built my team in such a way that I was able to retire from my practice, and it continues to be successful year after year—*without me.* My next goal—which will definitely require a huge leap outside of my comfort zone—is to completely rewrite the narrative for physicians everywhere. To bring us to a point where living life and practicing medicine on our terms is the new normal.

These things all bring me great joy personally, but my business and this book are not about me. I do what I do as a service to the physician community. And I've gathered together some of the best and brightest of those physician entrepreneurs to show you what *you* can do.

Let the Doctors in This Book Inspire You

This book is a compilation of true stories from all kinds of doctors running various types of businesses in many different stages. Each one is a current student of the EntreMD Business School. They are all unique, but they share one important thing in common: *they wanted more, so they dared their fears and chased their dreams.* Every single one of these physician entrepreneurs serves as an example of what is possible for YOU.

Have you been feeling stuck in the same place for a long time, wondering if there's something more? Have you felt guilty because you worked so hard to become a physician and now it just doesn't feel like enough? Are you itching to see what else is out there, but the unknown feels too scary, too risky?

Doctors, we don't have to go with the flow of the status quo. We do hard things every single day. We learned the Krebs cycle; we intubate little babies; we replace hearts. If anyone can figure out entrepreneurship, it's doctors. We can create an alternate reality for ourselves. It's possible, and the stories in this book are proof.

I'll be honest: there are a lot of challenges in our industry—especially for those of us who own our own practices. Each of these physicians you'll meet in these pages is honest about the struggles and obstacles they faced—and overcame—on their entrepreneurial journey. But each of them is also enjoying life *today* while they work on making bigger systemic changes. They're thriving right now in uncertain times.

You can live your dream life and practice medicine on your terms—and I'm not talking about 15 or 20 years down the road. You can do it *now*.

Read each of these stories and let them ignite a spark in you to get started on your entrepreneurial journey—or take it to the next level. We're here to show you what is possible. We're here to show you there's hope.

I love being a vision board for the physician community. I love showing you what is possible if you allow yourself to dream big enough. I love seeing physicians win. I love helping them get what they want.

I'm so glad you're here. Now let's get started.

Dr. Nneka Unachukwu

Founder, EntreMD Business School

OLUYEMISI FAMUYIWA, M.D

Business Type: Insurance-Based Private Practice

EntreMD Business School Student Since 2022

Dr. Yemi Famuyiwa is a renowned fertility specialist and host of Fertile Talks. With extensive experience in reproductive endocrinology and infertility, Dr. Famuyiwa is dedicated to advancing fertility care through education and innovative treatments. Her passion for mentorship and patient advocacy drives her impactful work in the field.

Website: www.montgomeryfertilitycenter.com

A JOURNEY OF HEALING, GROWTH, AND PURPOSE: MY PATH TO CREATING A PRACTICE

The journey to build my practice has been one marked by ambition, resilience, and a deep desire to help others, and it began long before I entered the professional world. From early experiences in Nigeria, where the seeds of my passion for healing were planted, to establishing a specialized fertility practice in the United States, every phase has shaped my commitment to service, healing, and growth.

An Early Spark of Inspiration

Travel with me to Nigeria. Picture a young girl, wide-eyed with curiosity, watching as her father, a man she deeply admired, battled illness. My father's experience with surgery, which he shared with me in detail, sparked something profound within me. It wasn't just about treating an ailment; it was about understanding the human experience—the fears, hopes, and strength that emerge in the face of vulnerability.

Shortly after, my mother also needed surgery, and I found myself caring for her as well. Imagine the challenge of being the only one at home capable of changing her dressings, trying to strike a balance between the love I felt for her and the detachment needed to provide proper care. It was a delicate dance, and through it, I learned that true healing is as much about empathy as it is about skill.

These unique experiences—caring for my parents and balancing empathy with a necessary detachment—sparked my interest in medicine and taught me that healing is more than physical; it's deeply emotional. These early moments laid the foundation for my journey, and as I progressed in my education, I held onto the passion for understanding the human experience, particularly in times of vulnerability.

From Nigeria to the United States: Finding My "Why"

I knew that, to reach my dreams, I had to look beyond the limitations of my environment. Inspired by a government job fair, and my love for math and science, I set my sights on the United States. Each step—applying to American universities, adapting to a new culture, and fully immersing myself in my studies—was fueled by a powerful "why."

Why did I want to become a doctor? It wasn't just a career choice; it was rooted in a profound fascination with the human body, the science that governs it, and an innate calling to help others. This "why" became my internal engine, propelling me forward through even the hardest moments. My purpose was clear: to truly understand and support people through life's most intimate health challenges. And this purpose drove me to overcome every obstacle along the way.

This purpose carried me through my studies at Emory University School of Medicine, where I was drawn to many fields but ultimately found my calling in Obstetrics and Gynecology. The desire to serve, combined with the science and complexity of reproductive health, guided me toward infertility treatment, a specialty that offered both intellectual fulfillment and personal alignment.

Building My Practice: From Vision to Reality

Starting a private practice meant navigating an entirely new set of challenges. It began with a simple notebook where I listed everything I would need to create the comprehensive, patient-centered experience I had envisioned. With careful planning, advice from mentors, and resources from the American Medical Association and local medical societies, I gradually established my practice. I sought wisdom from successful peers and mentors who reminded me to keep costs manageable, build relationships, and avoid financial over-extension.

These practical steps were crucial in turning my vision into reality, allowing me to grow without losing sight of my purpose.

Balancing Career and Family: Seasons of Growth

As my practice grew, I entered a new season of life—motherhood. It became essential to create a practice that allowed me to be present for my children while also serving my patients. I structured my days to pick up my kids after school, often bringing them to the office where they did homework as I finished charts. The support of a part-time tutor and retired teacher allowed me to balance these roles without compromising my dedication to either. During this time, I focused on nurturing my young family and creating a work environment that would evolve as they grew older.

When my children reached high school, I found myself ready to expand my practice. We moved to a larger location and developed our own lab, ensuring the highest standards by obtaining JCAHO (Joint Commission on Accreditation of Healthcare Organizations) certification. This achievement wasn't mine alone; it was the result of teamwork. My dedicated staff and I shared a commitment to excellence.

Serving a Unique Patient Population and Giving Back

In response to the needs of my diverse patients, many of whom required specific donor matches due to cultural preferences, I took on the challenge of creating an egg bank. The journey to launch this specialized service required extensive research, attendance at conferences, and a deep understanding of the unique cultural values held by my patients. Our egg bank, which started on a small scale, fulfilled a critical need for patients who found it difficult to find compatible donors. Each milestone in building the practice has come from identifying and addressing such needs, a principle that continues to guide us.

The success of my journey would not have been possible without the guidance of mentors, and I feel a profound responsibility to pay that forward. Mentoring young medical students, especially those who share my background, has been deeply rewarding. I encourage them to find their own "why," to show up fully, and to approach each opportunity with enthusiasm. I emphasize that success isn't just about academic excellence but about resilience, attitude, and a willingness to go above and beyond.

Looking Forward: Embracing New Chapters

Today, I find myself in a fulfilling new chapter, sharing my knowledge and expanding my reach far beyond the walls of my practice. Driven by my patients' curiosity and questions, I launched a podcast, *Fertile Talks*, which has resonated deeply with listeners, reaching over 500 downloads in its first three months. This journey has also extended to television interviews and even the privilege of appearing on a show alongside one of my patients. Through these platforms, my goal is to de-stigmatize fertility issues, educate others on preserving fertility, and empower people to make informed lifestyle choices.

As an empty nester with more time and focus, I am grateful for the growth of my practice, supported by a dedicated team who shares my vision of expanding our services and making an impact. This isn't just any practice—it's a pioneering one. We've built one of the most diverse egg banks, achieved JCAHO accreditation, and shared our story on national news and reality TV. Each of these milestones is about setting new standards in fertility medicine, pushing beyond traditional boundaries.

You Have Everything You Need—and We Need YOU

To the physician entrepreneurs reading this, I know the challenges that come with stepping outside traditional paths and navigating uncharted waters. But your unique vision and expertise are a powerful combination. You're equipped to innovate, inspire, and break new ground in ways only you can.

Own your story, let your purpose guide you, and say "yes" to the next bold step in your journey.

Whether you're establishing a new practice, creating services that didn't exist before, or reimagining patient care, remember that every action you take has the potential to redefine your field. Embrace the challenges, trust in your vision, and dare to be the "unicorn" in your industry. This journey isn't just about business—it's about impact, legacy, and the courage to shape the future.

LUCIE MITCHELL, DO

Business Type: Product-Based Business

EntreMD Business School Student Since 2024

My name is Lucie E. Mitchell, DO. I am a Board certified PM&R physician, Interventional Spine & Pain Specialist and an artist. I am the founder and CEO of Phoenix Noir Designs & Photography, LLC. My goal is to increase your quality of life and bring forth beauty out of pain through medical education and mixed media art.

Website: www.phoenixnoirdesigns.com

COLLABORATE TO ELEVATE: THE ROLE OF TEAMS IN BUSINESS FOUNDATIONS

I was that mom who thought that I could—and should—do everything on my own. Otherwise, it would not be done to my standards. Then my life reached a tipping point. Everything started piling up at work, in my personal life, in my business, and with my kids' extracurricular activities. I knew I was in danger of burnout, but I tried to talk myself out of it. "This isn't too bad," I said. "I can handle this. Next week will be easier."

But "next week" was never easier. The piles of laundry grew larger, and my chart messages and incomplete chart numbers grew overwhelming. I was exhausted. I was frustrated. I was mentally, physically, and spiritually defeated. I stopped working on my art, stopped doing YouTube videos, and stopped working on my business. I was completely burned out.

Several friends and coworkers reached out to help, but my pride got in the way. "No, I've got it," I told them. "I'm good. No big deal." But it was more than a big deal. I was drowning. I decided to take a break from my business and just work my 8-5 and drive my kids to and from activities. I did that for several months. It didn't help. Instead of recovering, instead of finding ways to fill myself up emotionally, spiritually, and intellectually, I read 19 Stephen King novels. I felt more burned out than ever before.

I knew something had to change. *I* had to change.

A Team Makes All the Difference

After six months of worsening burnout, I saw a social media post about EntreMD Live. I had read Dr. Una's books. I had been a long time listener of the podcast and had even been a guest. "Why not attend?" I thought.

It was one of the best decisions I've ever made.

The simplest concept—you need a team—is the one that changed my life. I had avoided hiring a team for years. I thought having a team meant I needed a lot of money. But having a team was how I was going to *make* money—and avoid burnout and overwhelm along the way.

Dr. Una taught me that a team looks different for everyone. You can have a team for your business, for your home, your personal life, and different facets of your life. As I took notes during EntreMD Live, I made a list of who I'd want on my team. The first thing I needed was a team to handle my children's rides to and from school and sporting events. I could use that freed-up time to finish my work, so I could be present for my kids.

Once I figured out that team, everything else fell into place. I have someone to pick up my son from school, help him with homework, and take him to basketball practice. All I do is pick him up from practice. With those hours I've gained, I am able to spend more time cultivating my creative side, get work done at the office, work on my business, and be a better person for myself, my family, and my patients.

Everything Comes Together

I joined EntreMD Business School, and I have been celebrating wins in my personal and business life ever since. When asked how I can afford it, I tell people that it's an investment, and my profits have already exceeded what I paid for enrollment. I've had more commissions for artwork, more contracts for my art with various companies, and have been able to do consulting in my specialty across the US, allowing me to travel more and network. I plan to continue to secure contracts for my art, speaking engagements, and expertise in my specialty.

As my business grows and evolves, I continue to build my team. I've learned to ask important questions like: What is the purpose of my team? How can they help me be more productive? Which tasks can I delegate to my team to allow me to focus on revenue-generating activities?

It hasn't always been easy. Things didn't just fall into my lap. I've had my share of doubts, but I'm learning to trust that God has given me everything I need to succeed. Once I found that deeper connection and began to understand what I needed to do, I was able to implement my vision and get the work done.

Everything isn't perfect. Things don't always happen as fast as I'd like. My team is not yet complete. There is always something else to do, another level to achieve. One of the biggest lessons I've learned thus far is giving myself grace.

As women, we tend to be so hard on ourselves. We feel like we have to do the absolute most—and that we have to do it ourselves. "No one can do it like me," we say. But we can't DO it alone—and we don't have to.

We can make our big To Do list, choose the top three to five things we alone can do, then delegate the rest to our team. The freedom we get in return is so rewarding, believe me.

Build your team, give yourself grace, and enjoy the journey. The best is yet to come.

CATHERINE HARMON TOOMER, M.D

Business Type: Coach/Consultant

EntreMD Business School Student Since 2021

Dr. Toomer is a Family Medicine physician, certified hypnotherapist, founder of the Total Weight Care Institute™, and hosts the popular Dr. Toomer Talks Show. She took a health crisis and made it her calling by creating successful wellness and weight health programs for patients, and for training physicians in compassionate weight care to achieve their financial freedom and time autonomy.

Website: www.drtoomer.com

LIVING ON (BORROWED) TIME

"Time is a created thing. To say 'I don't have time' is to say 'I don't want to.'"
—Laozi

Time is a luxury we too often take for granted—until something reminds us of how precious it really is. The date was April 24th, 2001—one month to the day after giving birth to my beautiful daughter—and the day that changed my relationship with time forever.

My husband was out of town, and I sat gripping the edge of the sofa, gasping for air, while my mother-in-law unsuccessfully consoled my exclusively breastfed, hungry child. I watched my normally unflappable father-in-law frantically fumbling with a phone to call 911. We kept our voices down, so as not to wake my sleeping two-year-old in the next room.

By the time the ambulance came, my oxygen level was critically low, and my heart rate was unsustainably high. My toddler was awake and screaming for me, and I was rushed to the nearest hospital with my baby on my breast because I had no other way to feed her.

My diagnosis: postpartum cardiomyopathy with an ejection fraction of 15% and a mortality rate of 50+% within 5 years. So began the countdown and my love-hate relationship with time.

Time: the One Resource We All Have in Common

We each have the same 24 hours a day, yet how we use that time, how we experience it, and how it impacts our life differs widely. The distinction between "living on time" and "living on *borrowed* time" is particularly poignant because we sometimes cannot tell the difference. I half-lived five years knowing my time could be up at any moment. I under-lived another sixteen years feeling as though that time was borrowed.

After nine years of recovery, I finally returned to practicing medicine. Even though I was only employed part-time, the patient-load expectations, the electronic medical records compliances, the meetings, the evaluations, and the patient satisfaction surveys all became too much, and my heart bore the brunt of the pressure. I was reminded once again that my time on earth was fragile.

I walked away from that job without knowing what I was going to do next. So, when a small medical office with low rent became available, I took it as a sign that I should start my own part-time micro-practice. I could control my time, and hopefully I could also preserve it.

Although confident I could handle my own practice, I was worried about the execution. But I knew I didn't want my time owned by an employer. So I persevered, but with a lot of mind drama.

My Biggest Fears—and Their Solutions

Thankfully, I got help with my mind drama and was able to find solutions that put my mind at ease.

Fear #1: Success requires a lot of time away from the people I love. **The Solution**: Create a system to generate the most revenue with the least time currency within my zone of genius. In my case, a direct weight care subscription model practice.

Fear #2: I would acquire heavy debt in order to get my business up and running. **The Solution**: I took an urgent care position with flexible shifts to finance my practice until it could sustain itself.

Fear #3: I knew nothing about running a medical practice. **The Solution**: Enter Dr. Una and the EntreMD Business School. I joined the course, the coaching, and the community—and an entrepreneur was born. Three short months later, my practice was making a profit.

Borrowed Time Steals From Us

Since my near-death experience, I measure success by the ease with which I can control my time. Sadly, this was originally shaped by the fear that I didn't have much more of it. So entrepreneurship became a game of precision prioritization—a skill usually learned with experience and growth. In my case, it was a happy accident born from urgency. Living on borrowed time shifted my energy from strategy to survival. I was laser-focused because I felt I had no choice, but that early precision was wasted at the time.

I opened my dream micro-practice so I could approach medicine on my own terms and in the way I was trained: using a whole-person biopsychosocial model. Many physicians never pursue their dream because they are always looking for the elusive "right time." We often forget that time invested wisely can have a huge return on that investment (think medical school). We too often passively wait for the day when there is enough time for family, friends, health, travel, and self-care.

When living on *time*, actions are taken from a place of clarity and strategy. The feeling of living on *borrowed* time (it is a feeling, not a reality) leads to action taken from a place of imbalance, urgency, and unpredictability. This leads to creating systems and processes instead of actually implementing them. In other words, busy work that looks good, but gets you nowhere.

For me, living on borrowed time resulted in aggressively seeking peace, purpose, profitability, and social importance in business. For others, it might result in feeling guilty for spending time on one important thing or person and not another. Living on borrowed time is like racing against a clock, our time hijacked by forces outside our control. The best part of entrepreneurship is having time autonomy. When we live on borrowed time, we give our autonomy away to a feeling that isn't real.

During COVID, my practice went from a brick-and-mortar office to 100% virtual. Suddenly the feeling of running out of time became more acute. It took every coping mechanism I had not to live in constant panic and to go back to what was safe and familiar. My health suffered.

I knew I needed to find that golden spot between complacency and panic. My goal was controlled, directed, and productive urgency. Thankfully, I found it—just in time.

How I Have Learned to Control My Time

I am now a successful entrepreneur with complete time autonomy. I grow revenue easily through various verticals. I have purpose and peace.

How did I do it? How did I learn to manage my time (and therefore my sanity)? Adaptability and flexibility have been critical components to controlling my fears around time. Here are some other important lessons I've learned:

1. **Embrace imperfection.** Perfectionism wastes time and delays progress. Often good enough really *is* good enough. I learned to embrace the beauty of imperfection rather than repeating the same task over and over hoping to "get it right."
2. **Prioritize ruthlessly.** I call it the M.E.M.O. Method™ —Minimal Effort for Maximal Outcome—a no-fluff solution to moving the needle and not getting distracted by anything that doesn't feed progress.
3. **Live on time to control stress**. The feeling of running out of time is stress-inducing. It is important to recognize the difference.
4. **Learn to enjoy creative solutions**. Things will go wrong, and when they do, it's essential to find excitement in pivoting and to seek solutions in the mess. Do your best in a given situation, and accept the result.
5. **Know when to ask for help.** Know when you don't know what you don't know. Smart entrepreneurs know when to ask for help—whether it's from courses, coaches, a community, or all of the above. Asking for help isn't a sign of failure; it's a sign of intelligence.

In life and entrepreneurship, time is unpredictable. Sometimes everything falls into place at the right time and other times we're struggling through the mess. Entrepreneurship is a constant negotiation between the stride and the struggle. When worrying about not having enough time, the time you now have is less productive—and prophetically problematic.

Time passes whether we use it for our benefit or not. Time passes whether we enjoy it or not. Time passes whether we celebrate it or not. Time always passes.

Time autonomy is the ultimate in living on time and not having to borrow it. Time autonomy is also the best part of having your own business; It affords you the ability to buy the time you want and need. I found my freedom in no longer worrying about where I was borrowing time, nor how much more time I had left to live.

By following my entrepreneurial dream, I got on with living the best life possible.

VALERIE MUKANGA, DDS.

Business Type: Insurance-Based Private Practice

EntreMD Business School Student Since 2022

Dr. Valerie Mukanga is a general dentist, founder and CEO of Healing Wings Dental. She helps her patients regain and maintain their oral health and smiles so they can soar in life. For Dr. Mukanga, dentistry is a mission. She lives with her husband in the Dallas Fort Worth area in Texas.

Website: www.Facebook.com/DrValerieMukanga

SHINE YOUR LIGHT AND IMPACT THE WORLD

I never imagined that a simple childhood dream would lead me on a path filled with challenges, resilience, and divine purpose. When I was 10 years old, my dad asked me what I wanted to be when I grew up. "A doctor," I confidently replied, envisioning a future dedicated to healing.

However, before graduating high school, the political climate in my home country, the Democratic Republic of Congo, became uncertain, leading my parents to send me to the United States to pursue my studies. It was a brave new world for a shy girl navigating a foreign land.

Despite the culture shock and feelings of homesickness, I resolved to adapt. As a native French speaker, I began studying English as a second language at the University of South Carolina, later continuing my education at Tulane University.

Not an Easy Road

Misguided by my academic advisor, who warned me that it would be extremely challenging for an F1 visa student to become a physician in the U.S., I lost sight of my goal. Instead of pursuing my dream, I graduated with a BS in Biology and began working as a laboratory technician.

However, a spark reignited my passion for becoming a doctor, leading me to apply to dental school. Upon acceptance into the University of Tennessee, I left Dallas, Texas with a renewed determination. After overcoming multiple challenges, I proudly graduated with my Doctorate of Dental Surgery in 2011 and completed a General Practice Residency at Bronx Lebanon Hospital in New York City the following year.

With a heart full of hope, I moved back to Dallas, dreaming of one day opening my own practice. But first, I sought experience successively working as a general dentist for three different practices. Over the years, however, I grew weary of implementing visions that were not my own. My vision was simple: to care for my patients as I would my own family. Yet, as an employee, I found it difficult to dedicate the necessary time and attention to each patient. It became clear that I was ready to embark on my own journey as a business owner.

While fulfilling my continuing education requirements, I attended a dental conference and stumbled upon a dental brokerage company. They provided me with crucial information on how to open my practice. It was a revelation—I was ready to start the process.

I contracted a medical brokerage company that helped me find a location and guided me through the intricate process, leveraging their network of professionals. The journey unfolded smoothly, as if circumstances were aligning to support my vision. Within six months, I opened the doors to Healing Wings Dental.

Yet, despite this milestone, I was in for a tumultuous ride. In my naiveté, I overlooked one crucial element: marketing. I assumed that, as a skilled clinician, patients would flock to my practice. Reality soon struck me; I had not adequately evaluated my vendors. I had trusted a consulting company that advised me to set a low price of $29 for new patient exams and X-rays. This decision put me at a disadvantage right from the start. Pricing too low can lead potential patients to question credibility in comparison to competitors. Additionally, I relied solely on a direct mail campaign that was ill-suited for my neighborhood. My fear of putting myself out there—perhaps due to my identity as a Black woman—blinded me to the fact that my name already revealed my ethnicity.

By 2018, I faced the terrifying prospect of losing my practice due to severe financial difficulties. To stay afloat, I made the painful decision to sell my house. But from this low point, I embarked on a transformative marketing journey. It was then that things began to change, though I still felt like I was winging it as an entrepreneur.

An Introvert Embraces Visibility

As entrepreneurs, our vision is like a beacon of light. As my favorite book reminds us, we don't light a lamp and put it under a basket; we place it on a stand for all to see. In the same way, I resolved to let my light shine before others, allowing them to witness my good deeds and glorify my Father in heaven.

In 2022, a friend of mine introduced me to the EntreMD podcast. The podcast inspired me so much that I decided to join the EntreMD Business School on December 24th, 2022. This was the best Christmas gift I had ever given myself and marked a pivotal shift in my mindset.

From EBS I learned that my patients already existed; they just didn't know I was here. It became my duty to increase my visibility and establish myself as the expert I was meant to be. I had to silence the inner voice that labeled me an imposter, convincing me I had nothing significant to share. After all, my years of education, practice, and the positive experiences of my patients affirmed my expertise.

As an introvert, stepping into the spotlight felt daunting. But I embraced the challenge. I timidly embarked on this journey of becoming more visible by implementing different strategies discussed in EBS. One of the first steps was empowering my team to consistently request Google reviews and testimonials, giving our patients a platform to freely share their experiences. Our team also regularly visits other local businesses to share our mission and connect with potential referral sources.

I revamped my personal and business social media handles to reflect the essential truth: oral health is integral to overall well-being. This conviction deepened after losing my maternal uncle to a stroke caused by a dental infection.

Week after week, I began creating posts in both English and French, discussing various oral health topics. I leveraged the supportive EntreMD community to appear on other doctors' platforms, expanding my reach. I also pitched myself for podcast appearances, both within and outside the EntreMD network. Now, I'm even interviewing guests on my platforms to share tips for optimal living.

This journey has not only stretched me but has also boosted my self-confidence and broadened my audience. This increased visibility has opened doors I never expected. My family and employees have noticed the positive shift; I walk with my head held high. My receptionist once asked, "Are you praying more, Doctor? The phone won't stop ringing!" I laughed and replied, "Yes, but I'm also working strategically."

Over time, multiple families have joined our practice through networking events and social media, each with a unique story to share. One standout moment began with a local producer who said, *"Dr. Valérie, vous êtes partout!"*—French for "Dr. Valérie, you are everywhere!"—and invited me to speak on his platform. Not long after, a mother walked into our office with her four children, explaining she'd seen my interview and knew we were the right fit for her family.

Another unforgettable experience involved a highly anxious patient referred to us by another dental office. She arrived visibly shaken, overwhelmed by a past traumatic dental experience. Yet, as she was leaving, she was smiling and at ease. She later shared that her general dentist had praised our compassionate care and 5-star reviews. That unexpected referral reminded me how powerful it is not only to serve with excellence and empathy, but especially to position ourselves by increasing our visibility.

The Bonus of Personal Growth

My growth extended beyond my professional life. Listening to fellow EntreMD doctors who specialize in weight management, I transformed my negative mindset about weight loss medications. With the support of my primary physician, who is also an EntreMD doctor, I began taking semaglutide and lost about 30 pounds, significantly increasing my energy levels.

Being surrounded by greatness at EntreMD draws out the greatness within me. Interacting with doctors from diverse fields and backgrounds has inspired my growth. In this positive environment, where we turn competition into collaboration, celebrating each other's wins has become the norm.

Recently, a doctor from the University of Tennessee recognized me at a major conference and told me she enjoys my videos. In my Congolese community and church, people now say, "Dr. Valérie, I've been watching you online." I wake up smiling these days. My life feels more meaningful and impactful than ever.

I share my journey because greatness resides within you too. When you plant yourself in fertile ground and apply yourself, you will surely grow and bear lasting fruit. By adopting the right mindset, utilizing the right tools, and immersing yourself in a supportive environment, you too can shine your light brightly, creating a profound impact on those around you.

MAKDA MAJETTE, MD, MPH

Business Type: Speaker/Event host

EntreMD Business School Student Since 2023

Dr. Makda Majette is a board-certified Family Medicine physician with a strong commitment to public health. She has achieved awards recognizing her contributions including the prestigious Emory University 40 under 40 Award and Top 20 under 40 for Brickell Magazine. She is a professional speaker with expertise in self-care, wellness, and appreciating joy in life.

Website: www.instagram.com/docmajette

THE HEALING POWER OF JOY IN MEDICAL PRACTICE

"We need joy as we need air. We need love as we need water. We need each other as we need the earth we share."

—Maya Angelou

As Maya Angelou so eloquently said, joy is essential. In medicine, where the weight of our responsibility as physicians often eclipses our personal well-being, joy can feel like a luxury—but it is vital for healing ourselves and our patients. My journey to reclaim joy has taught me that embracing joy isn't just transformative; it's necessary.

The Elusiveness of Joy

If you saw my wide, dimpled smile showing all 32 teeth—including the wisdom ones (because I need all the wisdom I can get)—you might think joy and laughter were my natural states of being. That's partially true. Yet, for much of my life, joy was elusive. I had fleeting moments of happiness, but melancholy often settled in when I was alone. Even in childhood, a time many associate with pure joy, I remember nights of falling asleep on tear-soaked pillows and waking up to puffy eyes.

I learned to hide my tears, frustration, and disappointment because these emotions were not socially acceptable. I found curiosity about uncomfortable feelings was rare. However, my smile and laugh drew praise, so I leaned into them as a coping mechanism. I discovered that offering a smile or compliment made it easier to connect with others. Joy and laughter became my universal language.

When my family moved from the US to South Africa during my formative years, my ability to connect through humor and warmth helped me adapt quickly to my international school environment. While I believed I had mastered the art of bringing joy to others, the deeper work of holding on to it for myself remained incomplete. However, it was this passion I had for connection and improving the human condition that ultimately led me to pursue a career in medicine.

The Challenges of Finding Joy in Medicine

Fast forward to my medical career. I believed healing, hope, and happiness were intertwined. After years of rigorous training, I became a board-certified, independently practicing physician. On paper, I had "made it." But beneath the surface in that first year after completing my residency, self-doubt lingered. Despite graduating with awards, I questioned my abilities and place in medicine. Childhood insecurities resurfaced, along with a nagging question: *Is there room for joy in the practice of medicine?*

The more I tried to fit the mold of what I thought a doctor should be, the more joy seemed to slip away from me. It wasn't until I embraced my unique qualities, and connected with patients authentically, that I began to reclaim it.

A patient once came to visit me, anxious and withdrawn, on the verge of tears. I noticed she had an interest in my betta fish screensaver, so I told her about Max, the betta fish I had in medical school. Her expression softened, she laughed quietly, and exclaimed her love for the beautiful, majestic fish. As we continued the visit, and I listened to her concerns, she remarked how much better she felt both physically and emotionally. It was a simple reminder that, sometimes, a little warmth, humor, and authenticity can go a long way.

But these hopeful stories were not the norm. I had dreamed of establishing meaningful patient connections, solving complex diagnoses, and achieving a sense of fulfillment. Instead, I found myself navigating a flawed healthcare system that demanded machine-like efficiency: 20-30+ patients a day, limited face-to-face time, and mounting administrative burdens. Insurance companies and administrators often dictated clinical decisions, while electronic medical records consumed hours that could have been better spent with patients—or on self-care.

I also underestimated the emotional toll of medicine. I often carried the weight of my patients' struggles home with me, lying awake at night worrying about their well-being. Over time, the lack of sleep and moral injury led to deep dissatisfaction.

Choosing Change

My body and mind refused to let me continue practicing in a way that drained me. I had to redefine what fulfillment looked like in my career. While salary alone was never my primary motivator, I realized true fulfillment meant leaving the office each day with a sense of purpose and accomplishment—without sacrificing my health or family time.

During a break from work, I focused on my well-being. I established a regular sleep schedule, managed stress, and reconnected with my passions, like improv comedy. Taking an improv class was transformative. It reignited my love for laughter, sharpened my listening skills, and helped quiet my overthinking mind. Counseling taught me to challenge self-critical thoughts, replacing them with self-compassion and grace.

Spirituality has always been a core value of mine, and I learned to be more intentional about reconnecting with my higher power. Society often views physicians as near-divine due to our role in healing, but it is essential to remember our humanity. I love the phrase "*Physicians have an M.D. not a G.O.D.*" as a reminder that many things are still outside of our control and there is a higher power who cares for us and all of our patients. Reconnecting with my spirituality and asking for guidance from my divine helper gives me comfort and clarity, especially in challenging times.

Intentional care for my physical, emotional, and spiritual health restored my love for medicine and allowed me to explore how physicians can thrive in practices outside of traditional models.

Embracing Entrepreneurship

With my renewed sense of purpose, I sought new ways to align my career with my values. I examined physician entrepreneurship as a pathway to rediscovering joy. I was inspired by physicians forging unique paths: opening direct primary care practices, becoming health coaches, consulting for various industries, and more. Learning about these possibilities was liberating.

I began experimenting with intrapreneurship, public speaking, and brand-building as an employed physician. Visibility has its challenges, especially for someone who fears being seen. But I adopted the mantra: *"Feel the fear and do it anyway."* With the support of the EntreMD Business School community, I found the courage to pursue these endeavors. Their guidance helped me celebrate wins—big and small.

Practical Tips for Reclaiming Joy

This journey taught me that the hypercritical survival mode that got me through medical training was unsustainable in the long run. Neglecting my well-being wasn't a badge of honor; it was a recipe for burnout. Physicians are inherently resilient, but resilience alone isn't enough to help us thrive in a flawed healthcare system. We must adapt, set boundaries, and align our careers with our values.

In reclaiming my joy, I've learned to prioritize self-care, embrace authenticity, and pursue opportunities that align with my passions. Whether it's through patient care, public speaking, or entrepreneurial ventures, I aim to make a meaningful difference without sacrificing myself in the process.

I have found some simple ways to bring joy back into my life each day. Maybe they'll work for you too. No matter where you are on your journey, now is the perfect time to implement them.

1. **Build a Joy Habit:** Like brushing your teeth, joy is a habit that requires daily renewal. Look for moments of joy in unexpected places. When you can't find it, create it.
2. **Ask for Help:** Seeking support from mental health professionals, coaches, or trusted colleagues is a sign of strength, not a weakness.

3. **Let Go of Comparison and Perfection:** Your path to joy is uniquely yours. Release guilt and shame, and focus on what fulfills you. Not everyone enjoys massages and mani-pedis. Maybe your joy will be found in nature, reading a novel, calling a friend, or scheduling one minute of laughter.
4. **Celebrate Wins:** Acknowledge the smallest victories—they're stepping stones to greater joy. Many of us are quick to fixate on areas that we want to improve or critique, and we gloss over the times we did well or received praise.
5. **Embrace Fear:** Every leap outside your comfort zone—whether stepping into entrepreneurship or embracing visibility—leads to greater personal growth and fulfillment or a learning opportunity. Feel the fear but move forward anyway. There is no bravery or change without fear. Fear is a necessary companion in your journey to success.

Joy is powerful, healing, and life-affirming. It doesn't eliminate challenges, but it provides a resting place between life's storms. Remember, you are worthy of joy simply by being human. You don't have to earn it or feel guilty for experiencing it. When you allow yourself to receive and radiate joy, you become a fountain of positive energy, enhancing your ability to care for yourself and others.

Reclaiming joy isn't just about healing ourselves—it's about fostering a ripple effect that heals our patients, colleagues, and communities. Together we can create a more joyful, authentic practice of medicine.

MARY LEUNG, M.D

Business Type: Coach/Consultant

EntreMD Business School Student Since 2022

Dr. Mary Leung is a physician who is board-certified in internal medicine, medical oncology and hematology. She is also a certified life coach who is passionate about serving physicians who are stressed, overwhelmed and burned out. Her mission is to help physicians leave work on time, so they can enjoy life and enjoy medicine again.

Website: www.shiningwithgratitudemd.com

HOW TO ENJOY PRACTICING MEDICINE AGAIN

By the year 2036, there will be a shortage of up to 86,000 physicians. This alarming statistic from the Association of American Medical Colleges is attributed to people living longer and physicians burning out and quitting.

When the Dream Feels Impossible

Most physicians choose medicine because they want to help people. They want a fulfilling job that makes a difference. However, the burden of working long hours, low pay, and responsibility outside of direct patient care can all add up to burnout. The reality is a far cry from the vision, and physicians are increasingly unhappy, stressed, and overwhelmed.

I was one of these unhappy physicians. I had dreamed of helping patients, treating their diseases, and connecting with them in a meaningful way. Then came the shocking reality. I found myself spending four or more hours every day finishing patient charts, answering phone calls, and tackling in-basket tasks. I saw my last patient at 4:00pm, but my work day stretched into the nights and weekends.

Day in and day out, there was no time to rest. I was a charting machine, going through the motions of daily living activities. The resentment of working extra hours, the frustration of missing out on quality time with my family, and the lack of connection with my patients weighed me down. I was in survival mode, barely staying afloat. There was no longer any joy in medicine—it was a luxury I couldn't imagine. All I cared about was surviving.

Then COVID hit, and everything came to a screeching halt—including my clinic schedule. During the height of the pandemic, I was only seeing 30-50% of the usual number of patients. For the first time, I went home before 5:00 pm with my work completed. It was amazing. I had time to pursue interests outside of work. The little girl in me was jumping up and down for joy. What if I could continue to do this when my schedule was full again?

Hope Comes Peeking Through

Just when I started to have time to enjoy life, I stumbled upon life coaching for women physicians. I was not alone. I wasn't the only physician drowning in charts with no time to do things they enjoy. If I wanted something different, I knew I had to do something different. So I joined the coaching program.

Life coaching was the exact stepping stone I needed. I learned awareness of my thoughts, and this awareness became a powerful tool. I had believed that it was impossible to go home on time unless I decreased the number of patients. I couldn't see other possibilities until I started working on my mindset. I began to feel hopeful that there was a better way. I didn't know how to achieve it yet though, so I asked for help from my coach.

This self-awareness also includes understanding myself—my goals, my values, my "why." Understanding *why* you want something is so important. I wanted to leave work on time so that I could spend quality time with my family. I dared to dream and imagine a future where I left work at 5:00 pm with my patient charts completed. The more I imagined that future and the more I believed in it, the more I wanted to figure out how to achieve it. And I did.

Filled Up Instead of Burned Out

Because I want to have a great day, be efficient, take good care of my patients, and leave work by 5:00 pm, I choose to start my day believing that it is going to be a great day. I share this belief with my team and remind myself of my "why" throughout the day. What a difference it makes to be fueled by positive energy! Instead of dreading the day, I'm energized by it.

I've also started a habit of celebration. Anything big or small throughout my day is worth celebrating. After I see two patients, I give myself a fist pump. The little bursts of pleasant fuel are powerful.

Several years ago, I could not have imagined that I could work full-time, see 25 patients a day on average, and leave work by 5:00 pm. What I believed has become my reality. I am beyond grateful for this transformation, so much so that I am using my spare time to help other physicians experience that transformation too.

It is possible to get out of survival mode and find joy in medicine again. Know what brings you joy at work, then decide and believe that it is possible to achieve. Be well-rested before you start your day. Decide how you want to feel about your day, and use that energy to focus, minimize distractions, and delegate. Always celebrate along the way.

Joy changes everything.

SHERITA GASKINS-TILLETT, M.D

Business Type:Speaker/Event host

EntreMD Business School Student Since 2021

Sherita Gaskins-Tillett is a board-certified Ob/Gyn, wellness enthusiast, and event planner who helps high achieving women rediscover their true selves, uncover their desires, and create actionable plans to achieve their next level of fulfillment. Her signature event, A Weekend For Me, is a 3 day cocoon from which attendees emerge empowered to chart a course to their dream life.

Website: https://bossladydreambuilders.com

PIVOT TO POSSIBILITY: FINDING FREEDOM OUTSIDE OF MY COMFORT ZONE

"We'll just find some doctors who want to work." These words from our CMO hung heavily in the air. My colleagues and I sat in disbelief.

We, the obstetricians in our practice, had been in negotiations with the hospital administration for weeks. We were hoping to improve our compensation and work conditions. We had a thriving practice with a stellar reputation. We had worked hard to build great relationships with our patients, and we worked well together. We genuinely loved our practice; however, we were significantly underpaid relative to other obstetricians in the area. We were only paid for the babies we delivered. This meant a physician could be in the hospital all night with a laboring patient or spend countless daytime hours with a critically ill postpartum patient and receive no compensation.

From the outset, we communicated that we would resign if a satisfactory agreement could not be reached. We never imagined the administration would allow five physicians to quit at the same time. Yet here we sat, facing that exact scenario. I was reeling from the shock. This was the worst possible outcome.

What Do I Do Now?

I had my life planned. I imagined retiring from this practice. How could this have happened? Our requests were reasonable. We were asking to be compensated fairly, treated with respect, and valued for the excellent care we provided. How did we get here?

And where was I going?

After the initial shock wore off, I started looking for jobs. No other practice in the area fit as well as this one. I felt lost and dejected. I wondered if taking a stand had been a mistake. Then I recalled the challenges of the previous 18 months.

I had recently married and started a family. Because of my demanding work schedule, I saw my daughter only two hours per day. I had missed many of her milestones. I lived on autopilot going from one thing to the next, never fully present. When I was at home, I was exhausted. I had the life I had prayed for but was unable to enjoy it. I knew something was wrong, but I didn't have the bandwidth to identify or change it.

My awareness shifted during a vacation. Sitting alone on the beach, I realized I was hearing my own voice for the first time in a very long time. It was screaming, "This is not sustainable. You are not well." I immediately pulled out my phone and started researching wellness—mind, body and spirit. Upon returning home, I enrolled in a whole life healing course that transformed the way I thought about myself as an individual, as well as my place in the world.

Those lessons came to mind during this crisis. I knew standing up for myself was not only the right thing to do, but it was also the only option that honored and respected me. I had not planned to leave my job, but honestly, I had been dreaming of a more humane, family-friendly schedule. I had graduated from medical school with a massive student loan debt. Jobs with less rigorous schedules would not pay enough to support my lifestyle and cover the loan payments.

At least that was the story I was telling myself. I had never actually explored other options. What if there was a job out there with comparable pay and hours more congruent with family life?

The Pivot that Changed Everything

Armed with an open mind and genuine curiosity, I began investigating. I discovered there were numerous opportunities for OB/GYNs outside of the traditional practice model. There were office-only positions and jobs dedicated to minimally invasive GYN surgery. There were part-time and three-quarter time opportunities. There was shift work as a laborist covering the L&D unit or a hospitalist who, in addition to L&D, covered GYN emergencies and inpatient consults.

There was a whole other world of possibility outside of the familiar confines of traditional practice. I went from being defeated and resigned to excited and hopeful.

Ultimately, I pivoted to a laborist position. As a laborist, I worked 12- and/or 24-hour shifts to complete 36 total hours per week at roughly the same pay. This was a significant decrease from the 50+ patient care hours and 10+ administrative hours that were weekly requirements of traditional practice. I had time for errands, doctor's appointments, and self-care. I was able to go on field trips and attend school plays. My quality of life improved exponentially.

This pivot was a game changer. What appeared to be the worst possible outcome proved to be a blessing in disguise. The implosion of the practice forced me out of my comfort zone, and I haven't looked back. It taught me to challenge the validity of my thoughts. If I had been so wrong about my career prospects, what other magic was I missing due to assumptions and limiting beliefs?

Pivoting freed me in unimaginable ways. I upleveled the quality of my questions. I decided not to remain in environments or relationships that were not meeting my needs or were out of alignment with my priorities. As a result, I have since made multiple pivots and plan to keep doing so as I evolve.

Currently, I work in a non-clinical capacity. I am also an entrepreneur. My business, Boss Lady Dream Builders, helps high-achieving women connect with themselves, uncover their dreams, and develop the tools, mindset, and strategies to achieve them. I want all women to know the joy and satisfaction of being the architects of their own lives.

Four Blind Spots that Keep Us Stuck

Too often we don't give ourselves permission to change. My journey has uncovered four blind spots that keep us stuck and living beneath our purpose:

We don't know who we are. Each of us is unique, a designer original. There is no one on the planet endowed with your gifts and talents. As a person of faith, I believe each of us is created on purpose for a purpose. You are not an accident. You are here on an assignment that only you are equipped to complete. You are infinitely valuable and limitless in capacity. Embracing this knowledge helps us stop playing small and placing self-imposed limits. When we know who we are, we are open to exploring the endless possibilities for our lives.

We don't know what we want. We are products of our environment. I've heard it said that our thoughts are caught, not taught. Often the expectations of our families and communities become the plans we adopt for ourselves. We allow others to tell us who we should be and what we should do. We don't spend enough time alone with our thoughts to ask probing questions like, "What do I really want? If there were no obstacles, what would I want my life to look like? How—and with whom—do I want to spend my time?" The answers to these questions help us begin to uncover our purpose. The ultimate goal of your soul is to become the person you were created to be so you can fulfill your life's purpose. Connecting with your deepest desires will lead you to that purpose.

We don't believe greater is possible for us. We lack knowledge of who we are. We tell ourselves that certain accomplishments are available to others but not us. We perceive others to be smarter, luckier, more deserving, or more gifted. We disqualify ourselves before anyone else has the chance to. The reality is we are all born with equal potential. No one is better or more deserving than you. You are worthy of every good thing this life has to offer. It is up to you to embrace that fact.

We don't have a plan. According to Harvard researchers, 83% of people have no goals. Most of us are living life by default. We do the same things year in and year out, never making purposeful strides. Failing to plan stunts your growth. It is impossible to achieve more by staying the same. Clearly defined goals empower us to make strategic plans and put us in the driver's seat. Plans give us the roadmap we need to take action.

You Can Have Everything You Want

This journey has not been easy, but it has been fruitful. My biggest take away—you are never stuck. You have the power to change your life and reinvent yourself. There is greatness inside of you. You have a responsibility to uncover and pursue it.

Spend time with yourself. Ask probing questions. Don't fall victim to the blind spots. Know who you are and what you want. Everything is possible for you. Dream big dreams, make plans, and chase your goals relentlessly. You are the captain of your destiny!

NGOZI UDE-OSHIYOYE, M.D

Business Type: Insurance-Based Private Practice

EntreMD Business School Student Since 2022

My name is Ngozi Ude-Oshiyoye. I am a Family Medicine Physician by training and co-owner of Apple Valley Family Medicine. I aspire to own the best practice in our region where the patients love to come and receive unparalleled medical care, and the team members never want to leave. I am happily Married with 3 school-age children. My true aspiration is to attain Time, Money, and Relationship freedom. And inspire other women to do the same.

Website: www.applevalleyfamilymed.com

THE REALIZATION OF A DREAM

Somewhere between 6:00 and 6:30 am—depending on how exhausted I was the night before—I open my eyes and my day begins. I hurry into my bathroom and get cleaned up so I can focus on getting my three beautiful children ready for school in a flurry of activity, then off we go.

After that, it's a mad dash to the office to begin patient care, problem solve, and put out proverbial fires in the office. Lunch is patient charts, meetings, patient care, or dashing out of the office to run an errand or two or three. The afternoon is filled with more patient care and more problem solving. The work day concludes with another mad dash to get the kids and head home.

Then, after I feed the kids and put them to bed, I end my day passed out on my bed exhausted—only to wake up and do it all over again.

Something Has to Change

That was my life six years ago. I was a successful physician caring for patients. I had a wonderful, loving husband and three beautiful children. But this was not what I had in mind as a child when I dreamed of having a family and owning my private practice.

I wasn't in control of my life or the trajectory of my destiny. It felt like I was driving at high speed with no seatbelt and no brakes. Even when I was doing what I wanted, I was always worried about what wasn't getting done. I didn't have enough time, and I was struggling to survive each day.

I was working weekdays and weekends. My husband, also a physician, had a crazy work schedule as well. We alternated weekends to ensure that one of us was home with the kids, and extended family pitched in, but it was so stressful. Our dates took place in the hospital cafeteria where he worked, and our "vacations" were quick and rushed.

We made it work somehow, but I wanted more. "This can't be it," I thought to myself over and over again. After a lifetime of schooling to become a doctor, and now I was missing precious time with my beautiful babies. They were growing up so fast.

Something has to change....

I wanted time with my family *and* a fulfilling career. I didn't want to choose between them. I wanted freedom—time freedom, financial freedom, relationship freedom—so I could live a purposeful life filled with happiness and peace. I wanted my business to thrive without me and serve the purpose for which it was created—to provide quality and accessible medical care to patients of all ages in a profitable manner. I wanted to spend time with the ones I loved without worrying about money or my patients.

I wanted to live a fulfilling life and practice medicine on my own terms. But I had no idea how to make it happen.

Then I Found Dr. Una

When I discovered Dr. Una's teachings, I knew it was exactly what I needed. She offered a road map to get my practice running independent of me so I could focus much needed attention on those I loved. She helped me attain true balance for the very first time and achieve a life of true happiness and peace.

I hired her as a mentor and have never looked back.

Life is different now. It's so much better. I'm still busy. I still have robust ambitions. But that's who I am. The difference is that I'm not struggling. I wake up now and have a morning routine—devotions and prayer. I still get my kids ready for school, but it's not a mad dash. I'm truly enjoying my family—and my work.

I average three to four days of patient care a week, and the overwhelm is gone. I have a personal assistant who takes care of administrative and scheduling tasks and has been a lifesaver. We have amazing providers in our office that support and serve our patients. We also have teams that support our providers, so the office runs much better. We're getting ready to hire an office administrator to get us to the next phase of business. I have someone who helps with deep cleaning at home and picks the kids up from school.

I'm spending more quality time with my children and husband. We take three or four longer-than-a-weekend vacations every year. My kids are still growing up fast, but I'm not missing it. I'm there for them and enjoying each stage of their lives.

I'm Finally On My Way to My Dream Life

As I look back over my life, I've realized that, when it came to my desires, I would always defer them until later. "I'll take that vacation and spend more time with my family after med school," I said. Then it became "after my residency is over." Then "after my business gets on its feet." I found myself years later with so many academic accomplishments to my name, but with a lot of ground to make up where it really mattered—my family.

I finally discovered that happiness is not a distant destination but a journey. There's a quote I love that says: "There is no road to happiness. Happiness *is* the road." I realized I needed to live my best life *now* and be happier *now*. Now is all I've got. It's all any of us have. I am so glad I figured it out when I did. My family is much happier for it, and so am I.

There's another quote I love: "Be the person you want to meet." The people you allow into your inner circle affect who you become and impact your journey. It starts with who you want to be and deciding to live it every day, no matter how difficult. It's about surrounding yourself with like-minded individuals. I am still working on what this means to me, but I am having fun figuring it out.

I spend more time now dreaming and vision casting what I want my life and legacy to be. I have goals for each of the seven major areas in my life, and I work to improve them daily. I listen to three or four audiobooks every month while I'm driving. All of this has been a game changer.

If you've struggled with any of the things I've shared about in my story, you can make these changes too. You are worth it. You just need to decide what you want. Surround yourself with people that will show you the way and encourage you along your path. And then muster up the courage to take the first brave step toward your dream life. I'm rooting for you!

SARAH STOMBAUGH, M.D

Business Type: Direct Specialty Care Practice

EntreMD Business School Student Since 2023

Dr. Sarah Stombaugh is a board-certified family medicine and obesity medicine physician. She runs a medical weight loss clinic in Charlottesville, Virginia. In addition to her clinical work, Dr. Stombaugh hosts the "Conquer Your Weight" podcast and creates online content and digital courses related to medical weight loss.

Website: https://www.sarahstombaughmd.com/

MY PRACTICE COULDN'T GROW UNTIL MY MINDSET DID

"All you need to practice medicine is a stethoscope and malpractice insurance." Once I heard that statement, it stuck with me. The simplicity of it gave me hope that opening my own practice was a tangible feat.

Nearly three years later, I look back at my decision to open a private practice, and I can confidently tell you—you will need much more than just a stethoscope and malpractice insurance. But it is still doable, if you are willing to learn and grow.

My Early Relationship with Money

Growing up, my family taught me the value of money. My father had financial hardships early in life, and he wanted to ensure his family never experienced the same. Frugality and hard work were taught as virtues. I learned to clip coupons, buy second hand furniture, and work hard to earn money. I was thrilled when I was old enough to start working. In middle school, I started babysitting at every opportunity.

At age 16, I got a job at Pizza Hut making $5.15 per hour. If the shift was slow, my manager would tell me to go home early, but I would beg to stay, offering to clean bathrooms or scrub floors. I loved earning money, and I knew working more hours meant more money. Through high school and college, I worked in a variety of hourly wage jobs, thrilled to earn money.

It was only in medical school that I found myself a full-time student, working toward my medical degree and not an hourly wage. Medical training was a whirlwind, and after residency, I took a job as an employed primary care physician in a large hospital system. My first job was exactly what I needed at that stage of my life.

There were nine experienced physicians in the practice who mentored me. Each month, we had a business meeting, and our lead physician would do his best to help us understand our reimbursement. But try as he might, it didn't make sense. The hospital had applied so many complicated equations to our reimbursement that my colleagues referred to them as "mathematical gymnastics." I longed for the days when I was making $5.15 an hour at Pizza Hut, because at least I knew what to expect on my paycheck.

Over time, I realized how important it was for me to understand how and why I got paid. I wanted to understand the revenue and the expenses. Most importantly, I wanted to have a say in all of it, but as an employed physician, I didn't get that privilege.

Launching My Own Private Practice

When my husband was offered a job in Virginia, I started dreaming about owning a private practice. I had been practicing obesity medicine as part of my primary care practice, and I wanted to shift my focus solely to medical weight loss. With the belief that all I needed was a stethoscope and malpractice insurance, I dove in head first.

It is actually surprising how little you need to start a telemedicine-based, direct pay medical practice. I launched with malpractice insurance, a business license, a website, and a Zoom account. I did not even need my stethoscope. While frugality kept my expenses low, there was not much profit coming in either.

When I had joined my previous employer, they were overdue for hiring, and my schedule filled quickly. When I opened my medical weight loss practice, I expected patients would pour in. After all, 74% of the American population is overweight or obese, and I was an experienced board-certified obesity medicine physician.

I quickly learned that, just because you open a practice, it does not mean you will have patients. People need to know you exist. They need to know what you do. You need to make offers to help them. You need to tell patients, referral sources—and everyone else—over and over again. In a direct pay practice model, you also need to know and believe your worth.

My practice started to grow, but the profits were still low. Shortly after joining the EntreMD Business School, I raised my hand and asked, "I think I'm low ticket, low volume. What should I do?" Dr. Una advised me to do the EBS puzzle, basically doing the math to understand what I should be charging based on my working hours, the length of patient visits, my overhead, etc.

I sat down and crunched the numbers and discovered that I was spending too much time with my patients—and charging them too little. When I was a busy primary care physician, I had dreamed of having more time with my patients. Now that I was the boss, I was making my visits unnecessarily long. Instead of having new patients fill out an intake form, I asked the intake questions myself. When a basic concept needed an explanation, I would give a detailed explanation during the visit.

I had to figure out a better way.

Making Changes to My Pricing Structure

The first move I made was to become more efficient. My value to my patients did not directly correlate to the time I spent with them. How could I provide the same amazing value in less time? I started using an intake form and made educational handouts for my patients. I scaled my 90-minute intake appointment down to 60 minutes, without any compromise to quality. I shortened my 50-minute follow up visits to 30 minutes. I kept my prices the same.

Then I began considering a pricing increase. The number felt big and scary, and I was terrified to share it with others. I doubted my own value and worth. I had been taught to spend as little money as possible, yet here I was asking patients to make an investment in their health. Dr. Una advised writing the number down on a Post-it note and looking at it often. I practiced saying it out loud, over and over again, until the number became less scary.

A few weeks later, after giving a speech to the Rotary Club, a member came up and inquired about working with me. I was terrified to say the number to a real live human, but I put on my confident face and shared my package with her. Without missing a beat, she replied, "Great! When can I get started?" I hurried home and updated my website, my new payment structure now solidified.

I Needed to Spend Money to Make Money

Even though I felt confident in my pricing structure, I was still functioning as a solo provider with a bare bones practice. In the name of frugality, I did everything myself, without support from employees nor technology. I didn't even have an electronic medical record. My practice was growing, and I was creating my own handouts, calling pharmacies, and faxing lab orders.

I began to realize that entrepreneurship was an entirely different game. I was no longer an hourly worker, nor was I an employed physician. I was a physician entrepreneur, and no amount of administrative work was going to create money for me. More importantly, doing administrative work was actually keeping me from making money, because it kept me from marketing and spending time face-to-face with patients.

If my practice was going to succeed, I needed staff and software to support my patients. These things would cost money, but they would give me the bandwidth to create more revenue in the practice. Within a month, I set up an electronic medical record and started interviewing candidates for a virtual assistant position. These two changes represent a major shift in my practice, where I was able to buy back my time so I could spend it marketing, seeing patients, and being a mother and wife.

The growth of my practice has been directly proportional to the growth of my mindset. Starting a business is easy; growing a profitable business is much harder. Success requires understanding your mind. What thoughts are supporting you and which are limiting beliefs? While frugality saved me money in expenses, the same mindset kept me from seeing my own value. It kept me from employing other people and tools to support me and my practice. After taking the time to understand and question my own belief systems, I have been able to design a practice that is not only enjoyable, but profitable.

When I think about the future of my practice, it is much clearer than it was a few years ago. I know my program is an amazing value, and I am charging a rate that supports a profitable private practice that can stay in business. More importantly, I trust myself as an entrepreneur and the CEO of my practice and my life. I know I will continue to grow and face challenges, and I feel confident I will evolve to be the person who can handle them.

ISABELLE AMIGUES, M.D

Business Type: Direct Specialty Care Practice

EntreMD Business School Student Since 2022

Isabelle Amigues, MD, is a rheumatologist based in Denver, Colorado. She honed her expertise by studying in Paris, as well as at Columbia University, in New York City. At age 40 she was diagnosed with stage IV metastatic breast cancer. A timely meeting with a non-traditionally trained practitioner taught her a different approach to disease where she experienced the power of meditation, visualization, energy healing, and love. Her journey through cancer inspired her to learn more about these alternative techniques and she now blends western medicine and eastern techniques into her practice at UnabridgedMD.

Website: www.unabridgedMD.com

I CREATED MY DREAM PRACTICE AND YOU CAN TOO

It was déjà vu all over again. I felt like I had moved back to France, but the views of the Rocky mountains, and the English spoken in our doctors' room, reminded me of our reality.

I had trained in Paris before I moved to New York City, where I repeated my residency and fellowship at Columbia University. One of the reasons I had moved to the US was that American physicians were passionate about their work and never seemed to complain. Being a physician was my calling and I wanted to be surrounded by like minded people.

But here I was, having the same discussions we had in France—about lack of respect, not enough time to see patients, feeling unseen by the administration, and a lack of control over our working conditions. We had all joined this institution because we believed in its mission. But it felt harder and harder to be successful at it, and the guilt and frustration were palpable. And, while our salaries were not the main reason we worked there, they were increasingly becoming a reason not to stay.

Physician burnout was a hot topic even before COVID-19. The pandemic brought us together for a short moment with a sense of common purpose. But this respite was short, and our hopes for better care and respect got crushed once we were back to a "normal" life again.

Two Very Big Shifts

During one of these frustrating discussions, my colleague joked that "we should open a concierge practice." I am French (aka Socialist, according to my kids), so opening a concierge practice was definitely not on my radar. I smiled at the remark, but then something started shifting in me, and I suddenly had clarity. *We were upset at the wrong entity.*

This wasn't about our institution. Our institution was trying its best to help us be the best physicians we could be. In the healthcare system, the money is in the hands of the insurance system. My father always taught me to "follow the money" when I wanted answers, and it's the insurance system that decides how much gets reimbursed for tests and how much physicians get paid. If we're "in network," we work "for the network."

If my institution (a good one) was having issues, there was nothing I could do about it on my own—at least not within the insurance system. I started thinking about what other options I had. How could I continue to practice medicine—which was my calling—to the best of my ability, while also enjoying my work?

I didn't have an answer yet, but it was brewing.

The second shift happened on my Vespa (yes, the cute little Italian motorcycle). I had just discovered a new podcast, hosted by a physician who was also a businesswoman. Like me, she was non-native and had done part of her training outside the US. And, like me, Dr. Una believed physicians were made for more. In addition to her EntreMD podcast, she started a business school for doctors. She envisions a world where physicians can create successful medical practices and become entrepreneurs.

I Knew I Wanted to Be Part of This Movement

As I drove my Vespa, I found myself steadily slowing down to listen intensely to Dr. Una's podcast. I ended up finishing the episode on the side of the road as I did not want to miss any of her words. She talked about how, as physicians, we do so many hard things. We've learned how to do arthrocentesis and lumbar puncture. We've learned how to intubate and operate. We have treated sepsis, autoimmune disorders, and cancer. Some of us have delivered babies. Some of us have done training in more than one language.

So of course we could also learn how to be successful entrepreneurs.

In a world where morale was low, and burnout was the word of the year, her voice brought me hope, and I wanted to be part of what she was doing. I joined the EntreMD Business School (EBS) that same day. I was not yet sure of my business model; I only knew that I wanted to be part of the movement she was creating. Within two weeks, I had clarity and gave my notice at my job. I had a path forward, one that gave me hope and would make me proud.

One of the concepts I learned in EBS was that of high volume/low ticket vs low volume/high ticket. I did not want to work for the insurance system, and the idea of offering the equivalent of a Michelin Star experience to my patients was appealing. I wanted to offer the best of myself to my patients and allow them to present their whole selves, not just a symptom or a part of their issues. UnabridgedMD derived from these two concepts: seeing the unedited version of patients—the full version—without needing to compartmentalize due to time constraint.

I had given seven months notice at my job and took that time to do some research while creating my brand. I read books on the direct care model, and met some of Denver's direct care primary physicians (DPC). In the DPC membership model, patients pay a monthly retaining fee to be part of the practice. There's no insurance acting as a middle man. Patients know exactly what they are getting, and the physicians get their fair share.

The proof of concept existed in primary care, but could I do this in rheumatology? Very few had done it in the US, but I was up for the challenge. Honestly, I wanted to find joy in practicing medicine again, and this seemed like the best way.

Building My Own Business

I spent six months working on my brand. I met all the DPC physicians that were willing to share their thoughts and concerns with me. I worked on my social media presence, at first reluctantly, but like a good student who understands the importance of consistency. I also created a podcast called UnabridgedMD so I could use it to drive web traffic toward my website. As I was still employed, there was no mention of the practice, but behind the scenes I was building my website. By the time it was live, my website already had some traffic from the podcast.

Once I chose the business model and its name, it was time to make sure I had a solid business plan and budget. Being French, I am averse to debt, so I did research to keep my costs low and found ways to do things quickly, cheaply, and efficiently. I created an LLC for $300 and met with a lawyer for $5000. I found medical liability insurance for less than $2000/year. I paid $500 for my website design, and I pay less than $400/year for my domain name and platform. My podcast platform costs $15/month and my newsletter is just $20/month.

I decided to finance my practice myself and found a high-paying locum position for two weeks a month. When my practice grew, I went down to one week a month. It didn't take long at all for UnabridgedMD to pay for itself. I was in the black from day one and made a profit in a couple of months. After one year, I stopped the locums and was paying myself the same salary I'd received in my previous institution.

I had created my own dream practice!

It has now been almost two years since I opened UnabridgedMD. Every day I wake up excited to work on it—with my patients and with my team. We have grown to four team members with two more contractors. My patients are happy, and they refer people they know to the practice. I have increased my prices almost every quarter to keep the pace sustainable.

To this day, I am still in awe at myself for creating this practice. My team and I have challenges every week, and we use them to improve the efficiency and experience for our patients, who achieve remission faster than I have ever seen.

Practicing medicine on my own terms fills me with joy every single day.

BRITTANY PANICO, DO

Business Type: Insurance-Based Private Practice

EntreMD Business School Student Since 2022

Dr. Brittany Panico is a board-certified rheumatologist in Arizona, Oklahoma, and Colorado Chief of Rheumatology at Summit Rheumatology and Summit's Gout Center of Excellence. As thought leader and writer, she champions patient empowerment and integrative care. Dr. Panico is passionate about advancing telemedicine, access to quality healthcare, and cherishing her roles as a wife and mother of three boys and a dog.

Website: www.summitrheumatology.com

CARVE YOUR OWN PATH TO EXCELLENCE

Physicians are hardwired to pursue excellence. Every milestone—from acing medical school exams to landing a coveted residency, completing a fellowship, or securing a dream job—comes with the drive to excel. But as our careers mature, that drive doesn't vanish; it evolves. We seek leadership roles, find new ways to hone our expertise, or, as in my case, develop a specialized niche in a field we're deeply passionate about.

But what happens when that burning desire to excel in a specific area isn't supported by your institution? So many of us carve out these interests, only to face bureaucratic resistance or institutional indifference. We're left with a choice: blend into the sea of clinicians fulfilling their roles and meeting productivity metrics or step out and create something new, something excellent.

Stepping out of my comfort zone to develop my ideal career has not been easy, but the rewards are beyond what I could have dreamed.

Shining a Light on a Disease Long Ignored

Like many physicians, I began my career in a corporate medical practice right out of fellowship. I relied on my coworkers as mentors and slowly developed an eye to see and treat what was not always obvious to others. Over time, the administrative grind took its toll, and I was faced with a decision: stay the course as just another physician punching the clock or take a risk and create something that truly sets me apart.

As a rheumatologist, I was already immersed in a fascinating field, but I found myself drawn to a specific, often overlooked condition—gout.

Gout is a disease that seems to live in the shadows, rarely given the attention it deserves. Throughout my training and early career, particularly during my time moonlighting at a VA medical center in Chicago, I encountered numerous patients suffering from this painful condition. Yet, their treatment plans were often incomplete and fragmented. What we did not understand at the time is that, by only treating the acute phase, we were setting the patient up for more chronic systemic inflammation over time. Patients would receive medication to control their flare, but long-term management was often incomplete. It was as if we were constantly putting out fires without fully addressing the underlying cause.

As I treated more gout patients, I realized that rheumatology, like cardiology, could benefit from a preventive approach. Why couldn't we prevent painful gout flares, the constant and chronic pain, and the long-term complications of gout? Over time, I developed a treatment plan that went beyond the standard protocols and limited guidelines. I didn't just focus on treating acute flares; I aggressively managed the underlying hyperuricemia.

The results spoke for themselves. My patients were not only feeling better—they were having fewer flares and experiencing improved overall health.

If You Don't See It, Create It

In 2020, in the middle of the COVID-19 pandemic, my family moved to Arizona, and I began practicing as a general adult rheumatologist at a local university hospital. I made it clear that I had a specific interest in gout and asked to take on those patients, but my request didn't gain traction. At the time, the hospital didn't have the capacity to provide the intravenous treatment needed for severe gout cases. Luckily, I encountered a growing stand-alone infusion center, and I was able to refer my patients there. It became clear that there was a need to treat gout patients in my community, and I knew that, to give these patients the care they deserved, I would have to make a change in my own career.

As the pressures of recovering from COVID and an increased workload wore on me, I realized that staying in this environment wasn't going to allow me to pursue the type of excellence I envisioned. I wanted more freedom, more autonomy, and more control over how I practiced medicine. That's when I made the leap to open my own practice.

In early 2023, Summit Rheumatology was born. Our mission is to be the most compassionate, committed choice in arthritis and rheumatology care, with a focus on patient-centered treatment and symptom management that aligns with their personal goals.

A key component of this practice is our Gout Center of Excellence, which I launched in partnership with the infusion center I had already grown to trust. This wasn't just a business decision; it was a passion project, a chance to revolutionize how gout patients are treated in our community. I proudly advertise Summit Rheumatology as a Gout Center of Excellence, both on our website and through social media channels, positioning us as the go-to clinic for patients suffering from all stages of gout.

One of the most empowering aspects of this journey has been realizing that, as physicians, we do not need a special certification to pursue excellence. Physicians are trained for years, often decades, to become experts in their field. Just like athletes perfect their performance through practice and dedication, we too develop more expertise by immersing ourselves in the conditions and diseases we treat. Often, we're told that, to be a true "expert," we must work in an academic center, conduct research, or have some other elite professional title. While that's certainly one path, I've learned that true expertise comes from continuing education, passion, dedication, and a commitment to achieving the best outcomes for your patients.

To build a Gout Center of Excellence, I had to educate myself beyond traditional training and surround myself with like-minded professionals equally committed to the cause. I network with other physicians interested in gout, collaborate with the main pharmaceutical companies in the gout space, and stay on the cutting edge of evolving treatment protocols. Rheumatologists are finally beginning to talk about achieving remission in gout, just as we have established in diseases like rheumatoid arthritis. It feels like a new frontier, and I'm proud to be part of the emerging conversation.

Find Ways to Set Yourself Apart

So, what exactly is a Center of Excellence, and how did I establish one? While the term can have various definitions, the core idea remains consistent: it's a team or facility that offers leadership, best practices, research, and support in a particular focus area. In healthcare, a Center of Excellence must deliver high-quality, easily-accessible services while pushing the boundaries of medical innovation. For me, this meant partnering with an equally passionate infusion center; building protocols that ensure seamless, effective treatment for gout patients; and creating a practice that provides not just reactive care, but proactive, preventive solutions.

One way we've set ourselves apart is through patient engagement. We use an online screening tool to identify individuals who may be experiencing gout symptoms. Patients can self-refer to our clinic if they have symptoms of gout, and we prioritize these referrals to ensure timely treatment. This approach highlights our commitment to treating gout at all stages, not just when it has progressed to severe, difficult-to-manage cases.

Gout is often misunderstood; both patients and clinicians tend to view it as a condition that only needs attention during flares. But with this condition, uric acid continues to accumulate in the tissues even when there's no pain, setting the stage for future complications.

Behind the scenes, we have streamlined our protocols to ensure that patients are receiving the most comprehensive care possible. For those early in their gout treatment, we simultaneously address flares and long-term management. Education is a key component of our success—every patient leaves their visit armed with resources to help them understand their condition and the importance of managing their disease long term.

For those with more severe cases requiring IV therapy, we've created an efficient, patient-friendly system. We handle everything from prior authorizations to coordinating medication coverage with pharmaceutical patient access support, steps which remove the financial and logistical burdens that often prevent patients from receiving the care they need. We also network closely with other clinicians in the community who see patients with gout, and this has become an invaluable resource to highlight our commitment to treating all patients with gout.

Building this Gout Center of Excellence has required networking, collaboration, and constant self-evaluation. Our team tracks patient outcomes, reviews our processes regularly, and adjusts when necessary. We also take the time to listen to our patients, incorporating their feedback to continually improve the care we provide. This level of dedication is time-intensive, but it sets us apart and is what defines our excellence.

I hope my story inspires you to carve out your own path to excellence, in whatever capacity that may be. Physicians do not need another certification or more letters behind our name to become a leader in our fields. What you do need is passion, dedication, and the willingness to stay at the forefront of medical innovation.

By building a Center of Excellence, you send a message to your patients: "You're in the right place and I know how to help you." That message has been transformative for my career, my patients, and my team. It's what keeps me pushing forward, striving for excellence every day.

NABILA NOOR, M.D

Business Type: Intrapreneur

EntreMD Business School Student Since 2024

Dr. Nabila Noor is a board-certified, fellowship-trained Urogynecologist specializing in pelvic floor disorders. Passionate about education and evidence-based medicine, she uses cutting-edge, minimally invasive techniques to enhance patients' quality of life. Based in Allentown, PA, she shares her expertise on YouTube and social media, establishing herself as a trusted authority in her field.

Website: www.drnabilanoor.com

UNLOCK YOUR INNER INTRAPRENEUR AND BECOME UNSTOPPABLE

I entered my first job as a Urogynecologist and Pelvic Reconstructive Surgeon with one goal: to become a trusted and respected physician and an expert surgeon. Fresh out of fellowship, I knew the path to mastery was not glamorous—it was built through relentless practice.

What I did not expect was that, within two years, I would go from being part of a bustling three-surgeon team to running the show solo, serving a vast community as the only Urogynecologist.

It was 2021, at the height of COVID, with staff shortages and constant turnover. Most of my classmates still had mentors to lean on, but I was alone. Yet, instead of being overwhelmed, a calm focus settled over me. I was ready to face the storm, one patient at a time.

I did not just choose to survive—I chose to thrive. As an employed physician in a large network, I set out to build a Urogynecology practice that truly made an impact. I trusted my training, leaned on my team, created systems, delegated, and became a master of time management. But most importantly, I became fearless. I operated three to four days a week, ranked among the highest-volume surgeons nationwide at my level, earned my board certifications, had my second child, and loved every minute of it.

After all, this is what I had always dreamed of—helping patients, growing, learning, and constantly pushing myself. My confidence soared as I evolved every day.

Then Something Shifted

Then the work became routine—comfortable, predictable, even mundane. That fire I felt in 2021 had faded. I was not exhausted or burned out, but I was bored. The spark was gone. I did not feel inspired, and I was not making the impact I craved.

Suddenly, I could not picture doing this for the rest of my career.

I was searching for that spark again, talking to colleagues and exploring opportunities within my hospital network—research, administrative roles, education—anything to reignite the fire. Despite everyone's well-intentioned advice, nothing resonated with me like the clear vision I had in 2021. I could not shake the feeling of dissatisfaction. I had a great job, a thriving practice, respect in my field, and degrees from top institutions.

So why was I restless in my comfort zone? Why was I craving more?

A Whole New World

A colleague suggested I check out Dr. Una's *EntreMD* podcast. Curious but unsure, I gave it a listen, and from the first episode, I was hooked. It felt like Dr. Una was speaking directly to me, sharing stories of physicians breaking boundaries, facing fears, and doing bold, unconventional things. I could not get enough—it was like discovering a whole new world, and suddenly, I was inspired again.

I decided to join the EntreMD Business School, even though I did not have a business. It felt oddly right—just like when, at age 18, I left Bangladesh and flew halfway across the world to the US for college. Or when, at age 21, I applied and got into one of the top five medical schools in the US as an international student despite warnings it was impossible.

I do not seek out hard things because I am delusional—I do it because I believe comfort kills dreams. Discomfort forces us to grow, try new things, and discover unexpected beauty. As Paulo Coelho said, "When you want something, all the universe conspires to help you achieve it."

I did not know exactly what I wanted, but I knew I wanted more—and trusted myself to work hard to get there. At EntreMD, I was inspired by other doctors building their practices, leveraging social media, networking, and overcoming challenges. But I kept wondering, *what am I doing here?* I did not have a business, was not burned out, was not planning to quit my job—but I was also not content.

That is when I learned the term **intrapreneur**—someone who innovates and drives change *within* their organization. Suddenly, it clicked. I had been an intrapreneur all along. Back in 2021, as the only physician in my division, I built a practice instead of quitting. Embracing this new identity reignited my excitement and inspiration. I was not stuck; I was evolving.

I became determined to uncover innovative growth opportunities within my organization. We faced challenges with patient volume after hiring three new providers, so I put my knowledge to work. I collaborated with industry partners to host patient education webinars, reaching out to women in my community. After discussing possibilities with my department chair, I discovered a hospital community liaison program, which allowed me to launch outreach initiatives focused on educating women on crucial topics like urinary incontinence.

Another Big Idea Takes Root

This journey opened my eyes to the incredible value of investing in myself—not just through traditional CME education, but by embracing unconventional avenues. I enrolled in a business mastermind course and connected with trailblazing physician entrepreneurs. As a natural extrovert, I've always thrived on networking, but this time I approached it with the mindset of a student eager to learn from those redefining medicine. Through these powerful interactions, it became crystal clear: my true strengths lie in speaking and education. I have always enjoyed teaching students, trainees, staff, and patients, but could I take this to a larger scale? Could I truly become a medical influencer?

The idea ignited something deep inside me.

I had always dismissed social media, thinking, "What busy doctor has time to post?" But when I started exploring it, a thrilling mix of discomfort and excitement sparked an unstoppable drive in me. I consulted our human resource department about hospital policies and boldly launched my own YouTube channel. At first, I was hesitant to share my journey, but I quickly realized my content was not just informative for patients—it was a rich source of knowledge for trainees and fellow healthcare providers.

I dove into daily posts on Instagram, Facebook, and TikTok, along with weekly YouTube videos on relevant topics. The more I engaged, the more appreciation and positive feedback flooded in. Podcast interviews and guest spots on other physicians' platforms revealed a startling truth: the staggering lack of awareness surrounding women's health, especially pelvic floor issues. I found my passion as an educator extending far beyond patients and trainees, reaching families and communities nationwide, even worldwide.

Requests for specific topics poured in, and patients loved sharing my insights with family members who could not attend their appointments. By showcasing success stories and behind-the-scenes glimpses into my practice, I broke down barriers and eased patients' anxieties, empowering them to make informed health decisions.

As I followed other medical influencers, I discovered a vibrant new world where social media became a powerful tool for education, advocacy, and direct patient engagement. With the right strategy, it amplifies our impact and strengthens relationships within the healthcare community. Most importantly, it reignited the passion I thought I had lost. Recognizing the potential of social media, I applied to be the social media chair for the American Urogynecologic Society (AUGS) and was thrilled to be chosen.

I realized I could not confine myself to my clinic walls alone. I began networking and presenting at national conferences—something I had sidelined after fellowship while focusing solely on clinical work. Embracing multiple roles pushed me to learn and adapt in an ever-evolving medical landscape, and I was ready for the challenge.

It's Time for a New Mindset

To embrace all these changes, I had to transform my mindset. I dove into books on productivity and time management—I had both young children and aging parents in my life and needed balance. I refused to let my career overshadow my family. Understanding the importance of mental and physical health, I learned to delegate non-essential tasks like laundry, cooking, and grocery shopping. Hiring evening help freed up my nights for social media work after a long day. I also took up martial arts, which has been invaluable for building both physical and mental resilience.

I became protective of my time, setting clear boundaries and being intentional about how I spent it. Gradually, over a few months, I noticed positive shifts in my mindset, energy, and enthusiasm.

While this journey is ongoing—some days are easier than others—I am discovering a path of self-exploration that excites me. I learned that success comes from discipline, not just motivation. Life's demands can shift my focus, but I stay committed to small, consistent steps toward growth. I set clear goals, embrace challenges, and view obstacles as opportunities. Failure is not a setback—it is a lesson.

Taking bold actions, I seize every opportunity, knowing that if things do not work out, it is just not the right time. I embrace adversity as a source of strength. Positive affirmations keep me focused, helping me overcome guilt and self-doubt. With self-care, discipline, and a long-term vision, I remind myself: I am unstoppable.

MONICA MINJEUR, D.O

Business Type: Direct Specialty Care Practice

EntreMD Business School Student Since 2023

Dr. Monica Minjeur is the founder of Radiant Clinic in Cedar Rapids, IA. The clinic specializes in Restorative Reproductive Medicine which aims to treat the root cause of menstrual-related concerns to improve health and promote fertility. The clinic's direct specialty care model creates the autonomy to collaborate with other professionals to achieve success and have a thriving business.

Website: www.radiantclinic.com

FINDING CLARITY AND FREEDOM THROUGH SIMPLICITY

It is the first day after leaving my employed physician job. I wake up at 6:00 am to enjoy the morning. However, for the first time in many years, I don't have a clue what to do with myself. Not because I'm lacking things to do, but because I'm overwhelmed by how unruly my task list has become.

As I prepare to start my private practice clinic, the constant thought weighing heavily on my mind is this: "Where in the world do I begin?"

By 6:02 am, the blanket of overwhelm is heavy enough to keep me from peeling myself out of bed. I can't stop the spinning thoughts long enough to figure out how I am going to face the day. Rather than let myself continue to spiral, I start repeating my daily mantra of affirmations to help focus my intentions for the day: "I am bold. I am brave. I am brilliant." The repetition helps me break out of the overwhelming cycle and just start moving forward.

Getting started is hard, but once I do, it gives me the calm direction I need so I can focus on taking one thing at a time.

The Difference a Daily Morning Routine Can Make

I think we often believe that a daily routine is unattainable. Maybe we've tried it so many times and it hasn't worked. If this is your story, I encourage you to give it one more try. Having a morning routine that I don't need to re-plan every day helps me to center, find inner peace, and attain clarity through simplifying what is most important on any given day.

Now, it hasn't always been structured the same. In fact, it continues to evolve with job changes and family schedules, and it certainly looks different during times of illness, travel, or increased stress.

In general, my ideal morning includes some sort of meditation or prayer, exercise, spending time with my family, and reading or listening to something to help with my business or personal growth. Another vital key to my day is making the time to write down my aspirations for my business and personal development so it is at the forefront of all the decisions I will make for that day.

When I start my day this way, I feel calm and relaxed about my next steps forward. And I have already had some meaningful time with my family before I tackle the huge task list in front of me. This has not always come naturally for me, and I still have to curb the need to check off each task on my list every single day. I used to think that, if I completed more tasks in a day, it meant that I had a more meaningful work day. I realized I was often just trying to chase accomplishment. Busy work doesn't always translate to meaningful work.

Being Intentional With My Time

As I continued working toward opening day for my new practice, I began to realize the importance of evaluating how I spent my time. I started to pay closer attention to which activities actually made a difference in my practice in terms of attracting my ideal clients, community connections for referrals, and generating revenue.

Being open to this continual feedback and process improvement helps me to focus on the activities that move the needle quickly to achieve my next set of goals. This feedback very clearly translates to following up with potential client leads, connecting with new referral sources, and producing content where people learn more about my practice. It also helps me spend less time on tweaking my website, scrolling through social media for a new content idea, or figuring out where each plant should go in my office.

Once I've identified the high yield tasks, I repeat those activities over and again to achieve significant results within my practice. Following this method of auditing, adjusting, and keeping the attention on my prioritized daily tasks has helped to create a business that, within less than a year, has given me autonomy to practice medicine in a way I never thought imaginable.

My business pays me as a physician working in the practice, but also as a business owner, while still covering our expenses and creating profit within the business itself to continue growing and expanding our mission.

You Won't Go Wrong with the Basics

Many entrepreneurs achieve great success from a very basic business model, but then feel as though they need to change direction with a "better" or trendier approach. We may be tempted to discard the basics that were working for us initially, in the hopes of creating something that fulfills our need to constantly improve.

The overarching principle I use to avoid this feeling of constantly needing to reinvent myself is rooted in how I make decisions as the business owner. I encourage my team and clients to do this as well. When given the choice between something complex versus something more straightforward and easier to reproduce, I almost always choose the simpler option for the well-being of myself, my business, our team, and our clients.

Do I still dream up new ideas and ways to improve certain processes? Every single day. Do I ever deviate from the principle of always choosing the simple option? Absolutely. However, I am very clear on the intention to make sure that the business not only thrives, but becomes an entity that lasts beyond my own aspirations. Sticking to simplicity has helped me establish a strong foundation in my business.

Choosing simplicity means that our clients have a clear path on how to navigate our services, what is expected from them in order to achieve success, and what they can expect from our team for the delivery of the care they receive. This is all done while creating meaningful interactions that continue to produce repeat clients, heart-warming reviews, and word-of-mouth referrals.

Pause, Prioritize, and Plan

The growth in my practice has been incredible, but I'm even more excited about the freedom I now have to create my dream life. I create my own schedule; I don't miss out on family events any more; and I have traveled more in the last year than I did in the past decade. I'm no longer consumed or overwhelmed by my daily tasks and have the capacity to dream for a brighter future for myself as a wife, mother, daughter, sister, friend, business owner, physician, and human being. My daily routine helps me to continue to become the best version of myself.

How can you move forward with creating clarity through simplicity? I would challenge you to pause, prioritize and plan. Set aside some time to think through your daily or weekly tasks. Focus on where your priorities are and observe if that aligns with how you are spending your time and energy. If there is a disconnect, where do you need to create more space for something that isn't getting enough attention?

Make a plan to start small and add in one thing at a time. This may be as quick as a five-minute walk in the morning before your day gets crazy or taking a five-minute break in the middle of the day for quiet reflection.

Eventually, you will find that you can get out of bed on those mornings when the blanket of overwhelm seems to weigh you down. You will create a network of routines and activities that can break you out of even the toughest days and propel you into the life you have always dreamed you can have.

SADAF LODHI, D.O

Business Type: Direct Specialty Care Practice

EntreMD Business School Student Since 2022

As a practicing OBGYN in New York for over 20 years, my mission has always been to empower and educate women. I am the founder and CEO of Femme Vie Health, a concierge gynecology practice serving patients in New York, and I have a telehealth practice for those in Michigan. While I assist patients in all aspects of female health, I focus on sexual and menopausal health as well as intimacy coaching. I believe that all women, regardless of their backgrounds, have the potential to live life to its fullest.

Website: www.femmeviehealth.com

THERE IS NO SUCH THING AS FAILURE

It was what I'd always wanted—to have my own office and to be my own boss.

It was April 2016, and I had just opened the doors to my new gynecology clinic and medi-spa. I had done everything I needed to do to get ready—found the right place, got an EMR, bought two lasers, and hired an aesthetician and a medical assistant. I loved my logo—a woman wearing butterfly wings with her arms wide open—and the space was beautiful. The soothing turquoise, green, and white color scheme resembled the ocean—calm and soothing.

Everything was absolutely perfect. I couldn't wait for clients to flood through the doors, filling my schedule to the brim. But they didn't come.

My Business Fails

Months went by and I barely had people trickling in. I offered sales, Black Friday deals, and coupons, but nothing seemed to work. I felt guilty that we were using our savings to fund my practice. I was in network with every insurance carrier but, because I was a solo practitioner, I did not have bargaining power with the insurance companies. I would get checks for a penny or a dollar. It was so disheartening.

In 2017, I took up a job with a nearby hospital and became their first laborist. I worked my shift, went home to nap, then returned to my office to see patients in the afternoon. This lasted for a year until it became too much. I couldn't make the math work, and I made the gut wrenching decision to shut my business down.

In January 2018, with my heart in my hands, I sent an email to the few patients I had and told them I was closing my doors.

Entrepreneurship is in my blood. I've always wanted to be my own boss and create my own future, but I didn't know how. After my business failed, I lost my belief in myself and my abilities. I was too scared to take any more risks with our savings. I tried to quell my desire for entrepreneurship by taking another job. While working at that institution, I realized I was done making other people's dreams come true. I couldn't take it any more.

I Want to Make a Difference

It was September 2021 and I had just left my academic job. I didn't know if I still wanted to practice medicine or not. I was so jaded. And tired of all the politics involved in working for others. I did some soul-searching and realized the things that drove my passion in medicine were those things that were not taught or discussed in OB/GYN residency or medical school: menopause and sexual health. While sitting in the parking lot of my son's high school waiting to pick him up from football practice, I decided I was going to put all my energy into learning and teaching others about these topics.

In November 2021, I launched my social media account that focused initially just on sexual health and later on perimenopause and menopause. I got pushback from community members who were shocked and offended. Many felt that sexual health was a topic that should only be discussed behind closed doors. There was shame, stigma, and taboo that needed to be addressed. So I showed up on social media every day to change the perception of what a Muslim woman "should" and "should not" be talking about. I received some hate from trolls, but there were so many others who were supportive—and grateful that someone who looked like them was willing to talk about sensitive topics like these.

My goal was to make a difference not just in my community but globally, so I created *The Muslim Sex Podcast*. Because of this podcast, I was able to reach a wider audience, educating and empowering women all over the world regarding sexual health and menopause. But I still wanted to create a business of my own.

Then I Found Dr. Una and EBS

For months I searched for a community that I could learn from. I joined two different coaching programs before I found the one that would change my life and give me the mindset, belief, and community I needed to start all over again.

I was in a small coaching group with nine other physicians when I first heard about EntreMD. One of the doctors had just joined the EntreMD Business School and talked about what an exclusive and elite group it was.

This piqued my interest because I knew I hadn't found what I was looking for in this current group. I began to research EntreMD. I learned about Dr. Una's podcast and began listening to episode after episode.

I finally applied to EBS in October 2022 and began my journey. I had no idea that the person I was to become would be so different from the person who initially joined the school. I was hesitant at first to be vulnerable with the group or share any wins. I didn't think I had anything of value to share with people who were so much further along than me.

But I learned from Dr. Una and the other physicians that everyone has value and something to offer. I learned to control my mindset and only allow uplifting thoughts. I learned to believe in myself and my dreams again. It was slow at first. Because my first business had failed—and cost so much money—I only wanted a virtual business so there would be no overhead or personnel costs.

I began with a virtual intimacy coaching business as well as telehealth. But I soon realized that most patients wanted to be seen in person and have that face-to-face relationship with their doctor. It took some time for me to see the value in opening up another business and overcome my fears. My fellow physicians in EBS gave me the courage I needed to give it another shot.

Try Try Again

In July 2024, I opened up my direct specialty practice. After losing so much money—and my self-confidence—I never thought I would embark on this adventure again. The love and support of my EBS community taught me to show compassion to myself, believe in myself, and to never give up on my dreams.

The lessons I learned from the group about asking—for referrals, people to work with me, people to work with me in a different capacity—have opened up my mind to all the possibilities of how my business could work for me and my family this time around. I have confidence that what I am building will have lasting effects long after I am gone. This helps me keep going when I begin to doubt myself.

This time is different because I'm not in business by myself trying to navigate uncharted waters. I have a whole crew of entrepreneurs in my boat willing to grab the sail if it starts to capsize. This time there is no failure, only wins and lessons. This time I believe in myself completely.

MARY ALICE MINA, M.D

Business Type: Speaker/Medical Practice

EntreMD Business School Student Since 2024

Dr. Mary Alice Mina is a Harvard trained dermatologist and leading expert on skin health. She is host of THE SKIN REAL podcast and co-owner of Baucom & Mina Derm Surgery in Atlanta, Georgia. With over 15 years of clinical experience, she is an invited speaker on podcasts, at national meetings, and is recognized for her artistic eye and surgical skills.

Website: www.theskinreal.com

AMPLIFY YOUR EXPERTISE TO GET THE MOST OUT OF YOUR BUSINESS

In March 2020, I owned a successful medical practice with my longtime business partner. We treated skin cancers in a predominantly older, Medicare-eligible population. We employed 18 staff members and saw nearly 1000 patients a month.

And then COVID-19 hit.

It was a Thursday night when I got the email that changed everything. My children's school was closing indefinitely. There was a mandatory "stay in place" order and my office was shut down as well. Life as I knew it had been turned upside down and would never be the same.

Instead of taking care of patients and doing what I loved, I was stuck at home with plenty of time to stress and worry about the future. My income plummeted, but the rent remained due, our staff needed their wages, and the bills had to be paid. This was a stark wake up call for me. If I wasn't seeing patients, I wasn't making money. I didn't *own* a business; I *was* the business.

I loved being a dermatologist. I loved my patients. I felt fortunate not to be burdened with burnout like so many of my colleagues. But I was stuck in a loop of trading my time for money. My handcuffs might have been golden, but they were still handcuffs. In today's world of ever-increasing expenses, ever-decreasing reimbursements, and more and more demands on my time, something needed to change. Trading my time for money wouldn't give me the life I craved. I wanted something more.

I Decide to Go for More

I didn't know what I needed or how to get it, so I did what doctors are really good at—I started learning. I devoured as much information as I could about real estate, investing, and physician side gigs. I listened to podcasts, read books, took courses, and became active on social media. And I found a gold mine.

I was amazed to discover a phenomenal community of physicians in the EntreMD Business School who felt exactly like me. They were creating things, educating people, building businesses, and generating income without spending more time in the hospital or clinic. My mind was blown by these physician entrepreneurs doing incredible things outside the traditional realm of medicine.

I shouldn't have been surprised. As doctors, we are smart and dedicated. We have sacrificed time, money, personal fulfillment, mental health, and physical well-being to achieve our goals as physicians. We're used to doing hard things. We made it through medical school and internships and USMLEs and late nights on the wards. So of course we would be successful in other areas. Most of us just didn't realize we could do this—or needed to do this. We thought becoming a doctor was the last stop on our ladder of ambition. But what if it was just a midway point and there was so much more waiting for us? What if we could take our brilliant ideas and turn them into profitable businesses?

While I was invigorated about my new entrepreneurial journey, not everyone around me was as excited. My husband thought I was having a midlife crisis. "What are you doing?" he asked me. "You have a great career. You love your practice. Why are you doing this?' Others asked, "Isn't being a doctor enough for you?"

No, it wasn't enough for me. For some, it may be, and that's great for them. But I was different. And you're reading this book because you're different too. You don't want a career that is just mediocre or status quo. You know you were destined for more.

I Discover My True Passion

After dabbling in real estate and medical legal consulting, I discovered my true passion: speaking about skin health. I turned 40 during COVID, as did many of my friends, and we were all experiencing skin issues that were new to us in this phase of life. "Why does my skin look different?" we wanted to know. "What's happening to my face?"

There was so much misinformation on the internet. Sure, you could find influencers and celebrities talking about skincare and what to buy, but where were the true experts like dermatologists? As much as I loved educating my patients, what if I could reach thousands of people—maybe even millions—with my message? In 2022, to meet this incredible need, I created THE SKIN REAL, a podcast, blog, and website for people to get real skin education.

When you first start, it's slow. You feel like you're talking to yourself and wondering if anyone is listening. Telling my friends and family about this new venture was often awkward. People assumed I wanted to be some sort of mega influencer. No thanks! I just wanted to create value for people struggling with the effects of aging on their skin.

Over the past few years, I have stayed consistent, posting weekly recordings and clarifying my message. I have met some incredible people and learned so much through my guests. I've also had the opportunity to share my message on other people's podcasts and stages—and I became an author! Not only am I creating value for the public, but this has been an amazing creative outlet for me.

I still practice dermatology. I still love my patients and my practice. But I also love being multifaceted. I love thinking outside of the box. I have built revenue streams beyond my clinical practice. Doors and opportunities I had never dreamt of have opened up to me. I don't know exactly where this journey will take me, I do know that it is incredibly exciting and has been immensely rewarding.

I know it's scary to put yourself out there, but you can do hard things. You can have an amazing and fulfilling career as a physician, but don't let that label limit you from trying other things. What if being a physician is just the starting point? What if you were called to do more? With your skills and expertise, how might you change the world for others—and for yourself?

If you're curious about what else is out there, if you're feeling an entrepreneurial itch, don't ignore those feelings. Listen to that little voice inside. Nurture it, educate yourself, read, and start to connect with like-minded people. The question is not if, but how, will you amplify your incredible expertise? There is a phenomenal network of physician entrepreneurs out there ready to encourage and support you on your journey.

TOLULOPE OLABINTAN, M.D

Business Type: Insurance-Based Private Practice

EntreMD Business School Student Since 2020

Dr. Tolulope Olabintan is a Christian, Wife, Mother, Family Physician, Life-Enthusiast and Co-founder of Livingspring Family Medical Center. She helps people live long and well because she believes the quality of life is just as important as the quality of life. She is also a speaker, Mentor, Writer, Teacher and patient advocate.

Website: www.livingspringmedicals.com

YOU CAN START LIVING YOUR DREAM LIFE RIGHT NOW

I never thought of myself as an entrepreneur. Sure, I helped my mom in her consignment store, but I enjoyed interacting with people more than the trade. I was employed and content—until I wasn't.

"Do it afraid" was the movement gathering steam in the aftermath of COVID. It seemed to pop up everywhere I looked—even the Bible, a book very near and dear to me. I was perturbed, ruffled, uncomfortable. There was something more I was drawn to do, *called* to do.

So, we started Livingspring Family Medical Center. Yes, *we*. My husband and I and our kids—ages eight and seven at the time—became a team. He was the COO, I was the CEO, and the kids were the advertising agency and hug factory—to help with the tough beginning seasons. We started with a telehealth practice that opened on the ground seven months later. "Care, Sincerely!" was our motto and came to mean so much to the team and patients we serve.

Three years later, we have served thousands of patients with our motto and culture of sincere care, echoing the importance of improving the quality and quantity of life. People really do thrive when they feel genuinely cared for.

Looking back, I have no regrets. I am in awe of who I have become. I am a product of faith, team, hard but smart work, and well-received coaching. It has been a journey, and I'd love to share some of the biggest pearls with you. I hope my story encourages you to take a leap toward that entrepreneurial fire in your heart.

From Self-Made to Team-Made

I originally thought my medical practice would be a reflection of me alone. I would be the one doing everything. I would be the only clinician and filling in as a sometimes front desk receptionist, medical assistant, and cleaner. I didn't see any other option. Hiring people required trusting them—and paying them. I couldn't afford either one of those things. So I did it all myself.

Thankfully, I had a mindset shift. What if I could increase my capacity by teaching others the art of caring for patients? What if I learned how to be a better leader? What if I started a book club with my team, documented SOPs, and began automating? So I did. I instilled our clinic's core values into our staff. I helped them see what "Care, Sincerely" meant, starting from the moment our clients are received at the front desk to their post-clinician care.

As Dr. Una would say, I began downloading myself into others.

I had to fight the mental drama of "what if they leave and start a practice next door?" Thankfully, I had homed in on the abundance mindset that there were enough clients for everyone. I kept my focus on finding ways to serve my clients better and faster. Since my shift from self-made to team-made, we have served 7000+ patients and have 1000+ five-star reviews on Google. In EBS we learn that, if you want to go *fast*, go alone; if you want to go *far*, go with people. That has absolutely rung true in my practice.

The Intervention That Opened My Eyes

I had pretty much mastered the "ask challenge" where I continually ask people to work with me. I ask to be a guest and for guests on my platform. I even ask for donations from banks. And I was getting results. We were busy with patients. But there was one thing I was ignoring: "the numbers."

I refused to look at my metrics. I honestly believed the money would just come. I didn't like having money discussions with patients as I feared appearing greedy. So I ignored the numbers altogether.

Then our COO asked a mentor for advice. I looked at my numbers for the first time and realized I had uncollected copays, invalid insurances missed at time of service, and insurance reimbursements that were lower than expected.

I knew I needed an upgrade. I scheduled time to get help. We updated our collections policy as well as other areas. Besides getting our numbers in order, we began working on our systems. We were creative and constantly thinking of new ways to serve clients better, then we'd replicate it through systems to make it more efficient. This helped us work smarter, not harder. We recorded training videos that can be watched over and over again. We met consistently with our team for vision casting and performance review. We signed notes and reviewed patient cases in batches. We paid a scribe so we could see more patients in less time. We hired virtual assistants for administrative work.

Systems build capacity and create efficiency. I know where my money goes now. Never underestimate the power of looking at your numbers.

Even with all of this, being an entrepreneur is not easy. There are days I have wanted to quit for so many reasons. Team members that overpromise and underdeliver. Fatigue. Money mindset drama. Time constraints. Having to hire, dreading the fire. Staff shortages. Insurance recoupments and denials. Administrative burden and signing charts.

I've learned ways to get through the hard days. I document daily wins, no matter how small. I let myself pout when I need to, but I put a five-minute limit on the pity party. I rarely miss a group coaching call with my fellow EBS students. Hearing others share their challenges and victories is so encouraging. The entrepreneurial journey costs what it costs, and we deal with it, because it's worth it.

The Magic of Triple Wins

Creating a successful practice where clients, team members, and the business owner all experience tangible wins—that's the sweet spot. That's what drives me as an entrepreneur: how I can make this work for everyone.

I want to see clients getting the healthcare they need. I want to see team members fulfilled on their way to their own dreams. And, as the business owner, I want to be compensated well for my services and see my business grow and thrive. This is the balance of entrepreneurship. And when it's working well, it's absolutely magical.

My dream life is still off in the future, but the version I'm living right now is still worth celebrating. I'm able to spend quality time with my spouse and children. I'm able to schedule self-care in the form of reading, meditating, and exercising. I resumed my passion for mission work after a 13-year hiatus, and I'm traveling on a level I never would have dreamed possible. I took two trips to Nigeria in one year, a family cruise to Mexico, and a mission trip to Honduras. Not to mention traveling locally for conferences both as a speaker and attendee.

My practice didn't shut down while I was off seeing the world. It ran without me. I don't have to wait for some far-away day to start living out my dream. I can start right now.

BRENDA DINTIMAN, M.D

Business Type: Direct Specialty Care Practice/Speaker

EntreMD Business School Student Since 2022

I am a board certified Dermatologist with 34 years of experience and the CEO of Dermutopia Wellness, a concierge medical and surgical practice with a holistic approach to skin wellness. As the co-founder of Dermutopia Teledermatology with Dr. Christine Shanahan, I have mentored over 12 pre-meds and pre-pa students to pursue medicine and telemedicine.

Website: www.Dermutopia.com

LEARN YOUR VALUES

I had no intention of being a solo practitioner or a solo entrepreneur, but the universe had other plans for me. After moving across the country with a husband and one-year-old daughter in tow, I had started my first job with dreams of becoming a partner with a successful dermatologist in a well-established practice. When it came time to negotiate my contract, my future partner was reluctant to sign the agreement unless I underwent special value testing and personality analysis. When he did not participate in the same evaluation, this should have been a red flag.

I left my three-year-old daughter and five-month-old son, still breastfeeding, to fly to North Carolina for an entire day at the Physician's Center for Professional Well-Being and Burnout Prevention as a physician and two counselors performed psychological testing and evaluation of my values and professional commitment. Ironically, I was not provided lunch or given time to pump breast milk during the eight-hour day of testing, leaving me physically uncomfortable and beyond stressed.

I tried to outsmart the answers by saying that I valued professional success, financial stability, and business goals, but the keen testing identified that I was very driven by integrity and loyalty with a commitment to individual relationships. It also highlighted that if I did not honor physical, mental, and spiritual self-care, I would be unable to be a good physician, mother or friend. This turned out to be a painful but highly invaluable experience in my life that led to key realizations about myself that I have carried with me for years to come.

I knew I needed to leave this unpleasant environment to start my own practice. My husband, who worked on commission, was very concerned about our finances. I told him I would rather work at McDonald's, eat peanut butter sandwiches every day, and move 50 miles away rather than stay in this job.

Embarking on Solopreneurship

This determination to leave fueled me, and on my first day, I proudly saw 22 patients. My practice had the typical personnel changes and billing struggles, and later, the stress of adding a full partner and other clinicians to the practice, but it was worth it.

When my daughter's Thanksgiving play at school was rescheduled, I was devastated since I had a full patient schedule and would not be able to attend. My office manager immediately started rescheduling all of my patients for me. "These patients won't remember you," she said, "but your daughter will always remember that you didn't show up."

Her impactful words reinforced the power of being a solo entrepreneur. I was able to adapt my schedule to my family's needs and, for the next 23 years I never regretted becoming my own boss. Years later, my daughter gave me the biggest compliment when she said, "Mom, you have always been a working mom that feels like a stay-at-home mom because you are always there for me." This is what truly mattered.

When Integrity Calls You to Switch Lanes

Then came the worst year of my practice. I lost my only brother, my mother, and my nephew all within a nine-month period. I felt fragile and disillusioned. I fell into the trap of thinking that selling to private equity would relieve me from all these responsibilities and allow me to have less stress and more time with my family. After one year of negotiation, I sold my practice, and within 72 hours, I knew I had made a mistake.

It was very difficult to be an employee after 25 years of being an entrepreneur. At that time, I really didn't know what gaslighting meant. When I tried to advocate for a patient with a billing problem, the CEO said, "You know, it's not the billing concerns you have, but how you're saying it, that affects us here at Corporate." Later, I found out that my patients' pathology was being read by a compromised pathologist, who had made more than 10% errors on pathology readings. The company refused to re-review all of them and told me to "stay in my lane." Clearly, advocating for patients was not their top priority.

One morning, two men in gray suits from Corporate were waiting in my office. They proceeded with a spontaneous meeting to discuss internal targeted complaints about me challenging the "status quo," all while my overly-packed schedule of patients waited for me. Sadly, I suffered a great amount of damage to my self-confidence. As painful as it was economically frightening, I knew I needed to leave as this environment was threatening my integrity.

At the very last phase in my career, I began this daunting journey. Due to contract restrictions, I could not send out letters and emails to regain patients. With the support of my husband, my children, and a few close colleagues, I started over with just one patient at a time. I signed a new lease and created a small value-driven practice, using a virtual assistant and motivated pre-PA and pre-med employees.

I focused on my values: providing the highest quality-care to patients in a compassionate manner; spending extra time with my patients, especially the elderly; creating a team that shared my values; and mentoring the next generation of clinicians. I dedicated time to mentoring, rejoicing with each employee I guided along the way. Twelve of my mentees have been accepted to medical school so far. I treasured each newly-formed patient relationship and felt joy when some of my beloved patients found me again. I was able to spend 45 minutes with patients who needed extra support.

You Can Do Hard Things

With my self-confidence renewed, I joined the EntreMd Business School with the hope of creating a different way of practicing and, ultimately, leaving a legacy. This has been a welcomed challenge for me—finding it is easier to hide in the comfort zone, but knowing that the comfort zone never leads to growth.

I found myself stepping into uncomfortable areas—posting and engaging on social media, collaborating live with other physician entrepreneurs on social media, speaking on podcasts—and overall, just trying something new every day. As a result, my home life and relationships with my children became better, inspiring the entrepreneurial spirit within them as well.

Here are the things I have learned from my journey:

1. **Reach out to colleagues for advice during difficult times and join online communities for a fresh perspective**. Nurture your relationships with your physician mentors. Don't be afraid to share your vulnerabilities with them.
2. **Don't settle for a work life that compromises your core values**. I was expelled because I would not tolerate the lack of integrity and the potential for harming my patients. It took courage to leave financial security and to leave behind something I had created at the risk of not practicing medicine again.
3. **Create a good business team**. A trusted attorney, accountant, financial consultant and staff with similar goals are invaluable as you grow your business.
4. **Never stop learning**. When you have intense self-doubt, consider getting coaching or counseling. Joining EBS surrounded me with innovative and courageous physicians to learn from and grow my business. I overcame my biggest limiting belief—that I was too old to start over again.
5. **Be open to having multiple phases of your career.** Although you may think that you wasted time at a job that didn't work out, try to see it as another "mini residency" in business or self-growth. Work compromises may need to be made to help support your family and financial situation, but you can strive to create a more fulfilling new path if you are adaptable, resilient, and willing to take risks.

Looking back, I can see how my struggles helped me regain perspective and focus on my core values of integrity, compassion, and pursuing the very best for my patients—without sacrificing my life with loved ones along the way.

TAMARA BECKFORD, M.D

Business Type: Speaker/Event host

EntreMD Business School Student Since 2020

Dr. Tamara Beckford is a board-certified emergency medicine physician, author, speaker, and CEO of UR Caring Docs. She helps women create stress-free dream lives and overcome burnout. Featured in Forbes and over 80 podcasts, she hosts the "Dr. Tamara Beckford Show," interviewing 250+ physicians on self-care. A sought-after speaker, she has presented at Vanderbilt University, and her content has over 3 million social media views.

Website: www.urcaringdocs.com

NEVER EVER EVER GIVE UP

I remember the first time I thought about venturing into entrepreneurship. It was the winter of 2020, two months before COVID-19 found its way to the United States. I was terrified of taking that first step. I had a picture in my mind of starting a virtual ICU with friends, or maybe even a medspa. But I had to ask myself—why did I want to be an entrepreneur?

I was earning well as an emergency medicine doctor. I lived in a great neighborhood. My kids were in a private daycare. From the outside, I had it all. I thought, "Why am I unsettled? Why can't I just sit back and enjoy the 'easy road'—the one where you work your butt off, and magically, your money shows up in your bank account on payday?"

As I continued to contemplate what kind of business I could start, I eventually settled on a Telemedicine Urgent Care. That should be easy, right? I was already an ER doctor, so it made perfect sense. Even better, I planned on starting it with a partner. We would do this together. At least I wouldn't be alone.

We were both scheduled to sign the contract with a marketing company that would help launch the business. I was off from my ER shift earlier in the week, so I signed first. She was supposed to sign midweek after finishing her shift. Then, I got the dreaded phone call.

She no longer wanted to move ahead.

Refusing to Give Up on My Dreams

I was crushed. But I had just signed with the company! I realized that I was on my own. I had no idea what I was doing. All I had was my imagination, but that was enough to get me started. Imagination creates the vision that fuels persistence. When you see a clear goal ahead, you naturally work toward it.

But here's the catch: no one else can see your vision as vividly as you do. Even when you describe it, others won't grasp its full detail or meaning. That's why you have to push through, even when doubt creeps in or others question your path.

Many days, I doubted whether I could be an entrepreneur. I was "only" an emergency medicine doctor. I thought I had no other skills. I pushed my telemedicine urgent care, but it never took off like I had hoped. I was exhausted from working night shifts in the ER, while hoping people would find my business so I could take care of them on my days off. I thought about giving up.

But there is one thing I learned: *entrepreneurship is personal, but it is never just for you.* What you build is meant to serve thousands, perhaps millions, of people. But your path to creating something meaningful will be littered with obstacles. You will stumble and fall—perhaps many times—but persistence is about getting up one more time than you fall. You'll feel ridiculous at times, comparing yourself to others and questioning your worth, but persistence demands that you remember you're running your own race. It requires pouring into yourself constantly—mentally, emotionally, and physically. It's about erasing self-doubt and moving forward, even if one day you cry tears of frustration and tears of joy the next.

Giving up was not an option in my mind. I dug deep into my soul and remembered the name I gave myself when I thought I couldn't get into medical school—Tenacious Tamara. Well, Tenacious Tamara was back. She had been silently cheering me on throughout the years—through medical school, residency, and my first job, where I moved across the country without knowing anyone in that state. Yes, I had to find Tenacious Tamara again because giving up was not an option. I had to keep the vision of success in my mind. Maybe it wasn't a telemedicine urgent care, but I was going to build a successful business.

We all envision wildly successful businesses. This vision is the seed. The next step is to nurture it through persistence—unwavering dedication to your dream. Fix your eyes on the goal, no matter how distant, and keep walking toward it.

Pushing Through Setbacks

There will be times when you feel like you won't make it. You may question whether your efforts will ever pay off. That is when you have to look around and find the support you need to get to the next step. For me, that was the EntreMD Business School. I joined the school and began seeing the blind spots I never knew I had. I was around some of the most brilliant minds. I watched as my colleagues, now friends, navigated starting businesses from scratch to multiple seven figures.

One thing we all had in common was that a setback is just that—a setback. It does not stop you.

I remember a time in my life when I faced a profound physical setback. A medical condition left me hospitalized for six weeks, deconditioned to the point where I could barely walk. I had to hold onto the walls of my home just to move from room to room. As I struggled, I wondered what my future would look like. Would I ever regain my strength? I even contemplated buying a cane.

But then, something inside me said, "No. This will not be my life." I decided that not only would I walk again, I would run. And not just casually—I would run a 5K. Six months later, I did just that and proudly collected my medal at the finish line.

The setback in launching my first business did not stop me. I pivoted to speaking and have had the opportunity to speak on large stages, like at Vanderbilt University. I also recognized the power of my voice. I can command a room. I can tell a story. I can inspire people to live the best version of their lives.

That does not mean life was easy. I was still working full-time as an ER doctor while building my business. My schedule was jam-packed. I worked overnight ER shifts from Sunday night to Wednesday morning. I would sleep during the day and spend time with my toddlers in the afternoon. If I had a speaking engagement, I would fly out on Thursdays, speak, and run any online meetings in between. I have run meetings from hallways in Milwaukee, near the beaches at Martha's Vineyard, and from countless hotel rooms across different countries. All to rush home by Saturday so I could start again on Sunday.

Persistence Is What Got Me There

My first idea didn't materialize the way I envisioned, but I kept going. My speaking career opened doors to my coaching practice, which opened doors to my telemedicine wellness practice. Both are doing well.

It's funny how life unfolds when you don't give up. This is the power of persistence. It asks tough questions: Will you build belief in yourself when it feels impossible? Will you push your hopes and dreams to the finish line, or will you let them die with each setback?

It is not just about grand gestures. It's about daily, consistent effort—what I call the power of the compound effect. Small actions taken daily will always outpace sporadic bursts of energy.

You don't have to take giant leaps every day. In fact, the goal is to improve by just 1% daily. I do this by posting on social media, making a livestream video, or sending an email to a corporation letting them know I am available to speak. Sometimes it means driving to businesses and spreading the word about how I can support them. This slow, steady improvement builds momentum. Over time, I've looked back and realized how far I've come.

This is where the magic of persistence truly shines—in the quiet, often unnoticed, daily grind.

Remember, persistence doesn't mean you won't feel doubt. It doesn't mean you won't have moments of frustration or exhaustion. I've given myself plenty of pep talks before entering someone's establishment to introduce myself and my business. It simply means you will not stop. You'll trust the process, even when the finish line feels miles away. You'll keep moving forward, even if you have to crawl.

In entrepreneurship, persistence is not just a skill—it's a way of life. Keep your eyes on the finish line; take small, consistent steps; and trust that every single effort is bringing you closer to success.

CONCLUSION

Wow, what a ride! Wasn't that something? You just met some incredible physician entrepreneurs doing some pretty amazing things. Hanging out with them and watching them grow and thrive is a literal dream come true for me. As the fearless leader of this phenomenal group of doctors, I had already heard these stories, but seeing them all together like that impacted me in a whole new way. We are truly changing the world!

As you read, I'm sure you noticed a common theme: this entrepreneurial journey isn't easy, but it's the most rewarding thing you'll ever do.

You have a choice to make right now: will you let these wonderful stories *intimidate* you or *inspire* you? Because it could really go either way. Hopefully, you're going to choose to be inspired.

Each of these doctors did a remarkable job of stressing how anxious and inadequate they felt when they first got started, but they didn't let that stand in the way of them pursuing their dreams. They dared their fears and went for it.

And as the CEO of EntreMD, I watched it happen from my front row seat. Seeing physician entrepreneurs make quantum leaps in their lives and businesses will never get old to me. I was born for this.

The EntreMD Business School is the only school of its kind for physicians who want to build profitable 6-, 7-, and multiple 7-figure businesses. EBS is perfect for someone who is coachable, committed, and willing to stay in conversation and communication. If you're looking for mentorship, accountability, and coaching, this is the place for you.

I talk a lot about a disease I call "learn-itis" that's very common among physicians, where we love to learn, but we're learning to *know* instead of learning to *do*. This book (and EBS) isn't about learning to *know*; it's about learning to *do*. Do you know more now than you did before you read the book? Of course. But the magic happens when you start *applying* what you've learned. And that's what we do in EBS.

It has been so beautiful watching my EBS students help each other navigate through challenging times. The entrepreneurial journey comes with obstacles. It's inevitable. But when they come, you don't have to face them alone. You can lean into your community and get the support you need. We also have a whole lot of fun together and celebrate each other's wins, both big and small.

In EBS, you'll learn how to attract new clients, generate revenue, build and lead an A team, and build your dream life. We're not putting our dream lives—or our families—on hold while we build our businesses. We're building dream businesses and dream lives concurrently.

My EBS students are part of a unicorn team of doctors who are building the most innovative, most impactful, most profitable businesses inside and outside of healthcare. They are literal Walking Vision Boards for the physician community. One of my life's greatest honors is to work with these folks. I'm so proud of them.

If you want to be a part of this one-of-a-kind community, we'd love to have you join us. Evolution is magical. Once you start learning, growing, upleveling, evolving, expanding your comfort zone, you won't be able to get enough of it.

I tell my students all the time: this is your one life; there is no dress rehearsal. This is the real thing, and you only get one shot at it. So hold nothing back. Give it everything you've got.

I'm rooting for you!

Dr. Nneka Unachukwu

Founder EntreMD Business School

www.EntreMD.com/business

Dr. Nneka Unachukwu helps physicians build profitable 7 and 7+ figure businesses by teaching them the simple, proven and timeless principles used by the ultra successful. She knows that entrepreneurship is a vehicle physicians can leverage so they can have the freedom to live life and practice medicine on their terms. She does this through the EntreMD Business School, the only school of its kind for physician entrepreneurs, the EntreMD podcast, a top 1% podcast, and her best-selling books.

Before starting EntreMD, Dr. Una started her own pediatric private practice, a practice she still runs fourteen years later. In her typical unconventional fashion, she built it as a true business, one that can run efficiently and profitably without her involvement in the day-to-day management.

Dr. Una has been a Forbes contributor and her company has been on the Inc. 5000 list of fastest-growing privately held companies in America for two years in a row.

She resides outside Atlanta with her husband and four children.

Connect with Dr. Una

Podcast	www.EntreMD.com/podcast
Website	www.EntreMD.com
YouTube	@drunachukwu
Facebook	@drunachukwu
Private Facebook Community	EntreMD - Physicians in Business
LinkedIn	@druna
Instagram	@drunachukwu

Made in the USA
Columbia, SC
18 March 2025

55333063R00069